THE HISTORIAN'S TOOLBOX

THE HISTORIAN'S TOOLBOX

A Student's Guide to the Theory and Craft of History

Robert C. Williams

M.E.Sharpe
Armonk, New York
London, England

Copyright © 2003 by M. E. Sharpe, Inc.

All rights reserved. No part of this book may be reproduced in any form
without written permission from the publisher, M. E. Sharpe, Inc.,
80 Business Park Drive, Armonk, New York 10504.

The author gratefully acknowledges these publishers for permission to reprint excerpts
from the following works: *American Slavery, 1619–1877* by Peter Kolchin,
copyright © 1993 by Peter Kolchin. Reprinted by permission of Hill & Wang
a division of Farrar, Straus and Giroux, LLC; *Battle Cry of Freedom: The Era of the Civil
War* by James M. McPherson, copyright © 1988 by Oxford University Press, Inc.
Used by permission of Oxford University Press, Inc.; *Dead Certainties
(Unwarranted Speculations)* by Simon Schama, copyright © 1992 by Vintage.
Used by permission of Sterling Lord Literistic, Inc.

Library of Congress Cataloging-in-Publication Data

Williams, Robert Chadwell, 1938–
   The historian's toolbox : a student's guide to the theory and craft of history / Robert C.
Williams.
     p. cm.
   Includes bibliographical references (p.) and index.
   ISBN 0-7656-1092-2 (cloth: alk. paper) — ISBN 0-7656-1093-0 (pbk.: alk. paper)
     1. History—Methodology. 2. History—Study and teaching. 3. Historiography.
   4. History—Research. I. Title.

   D16.W62 2003
   907'.2—dc21

                                                                    2002030897

Printed in the United States of America

The paper used in this publication meets the minimum requirements of
American National Standard for Information Sciences
Permanence of Paper for Printed Library Materials,
ANSI Z 39.48-1984.

BM (c)   10   9   8   7   6   5   4   3   2   1
BM (p)   10   9   8   7   6   5   4   3

History as a Discussion Without End

You come late. When you arrive, others have long preceded you, and they are engaged in a heated discussion, a discussion too heated for them to pause and tell you exactly what it is about. In fact, the discussion had already begun long before any of them got there, so that no one present is qualified to retrace for you all the steps that had gone before. You listen for a while, until you decide that you have caught the tenor of the argument; then you put in your oar. Someone answers you; you answer her; another comes to your defense; another aligns herself against you, to either the embarrassment or gratification of your opponent, depending upon the quality of your ally's assistance. However the discussion is interminable. The hour grows late, you must depart. And you do depart, with the discussion still vigorously in progress.

—Kenneth Burke, *The Philosophy of Literary Form*

Contents

Illustrations and Tables

Illustrations

Tables

History as Fun

History is fun, even though the past offers us much tragedy, as well as comedy and farce. History involves the study of the past. History is not really an art, nor a science, but a *craft*. The craft of doing history—as opposed to reading history—involves a further intellectual process of research, writing, and revision. Doing history is hard work and requires tools of the trade. The purpose of this book is to help history students, and even other historians, understand the *tools* of the intellectual process and craft that is history. The tools in the toolbox (part II) provide a number of techniques common to reading, research, and writing, as well as some current controversies in the historical profession. These are simply my personal reflections and selections, with the usual limits of race, class, and gender. But they at least reflect the hindsight of a practitioner of the craft.

Forty years ago, I turned away from studying science to doing history with the view that history was a subtle, complex, and endlessly fascinating way of understanding the human condition over time. Today I still believe that to be the case. What I have learned about history has come from reading, writing, and doing my own research. There is no better way to understand a craft than to pursue it yourself. Most people, of course, are not professional historians. But they may be quite fascinated with reading history, seeing historical films, and visiting historical sites. History is all around us and speaks to us all. We all do some history every day without realizing it. But doing history professionally is another matter.

Looking at the evolution of history as a craft, I believe that history is here to stay. History will survive even the assaults of antihistory and postmodernism, of fictional history and "what if?" speculation. Telling true stories about the human past is an inherent part of human culture. So is simple curiosity about what actually happened in the past, and why. One ignores history at one's peril. For history can help us understand not just the past, but the present and the future as well.

History is an argument without end, as Dutch historian Peter Geyl put it. The controversies are never really over. (A former colleague of mine once said that history is what any six dead people agree on.) Thus historical revision—the modification of conventional wisdom based on new interpretations or new evidence—is a permanent characteristic of doing history. Historians often disagree about their interpretation of the past, even when looking at the same body of evidence.

As I have revised my own views of history over the years, I owe a great deal to my colleagues and students at Harvard University, Williams College, Washington University in St. Louis, and Davidson College. They all have taught me as much as I have taught them. And they challenge me to rethink history every semester. I am also grateful to Phil Cantelon and my colleagues at History Associates Incorporated, who have proven that history can be both professional and useful in the marketplace. My debt to Ann Williams is immeasurable. And my editor, Andrew Gyory, has made this book better than it might have been.

The year 2001 was once the subject of a popular film about future space travel. Now 2001 is history. Today's history was yesterday's future. So what is the craft of history? And what are its tools? What does it mean to try to narrate and explain what happened in the past? By confronting those questions, this book serves as a guide to understanding the purpose of history, the evolution of historical thought, and how the tools of history can be identified and used.

For Further Reading

Good recent general introductions to the study of history include Mark T. Gilderhus, *History and Historians: A Historiographical Introduction* (Upper Saddle River, NJ: Prentice Hall, 2000); Jules R. Benjamin, *A Student's Guide to History* (Boston: Bedford Books, 1998); and

Norman J. Wilson, *History in Crisis? Recent Directions in Histori-ography* (Upper Saddle River, NJ: Prentice Hall, 1999).

Another good introduction is John Tosh, *The Pursuit of History: Aims, Methods, and New Directions in the Study of Modern History*, 2d ed. (London and New York: Longman, 1991). Then there is the dated, but still useful, E.H. Carr, *What Is History?* (New York: Alfred A. Knopf, 1961).

Part I

The Craft of History

1

The Past

The past is never dead; it is not even past.

—William Faulkner

The past does speak through the sources and is recoverable through them. There is a qualitative difference between documents written in the past, by living people, for their own purposes, and later interpretations advanced about the past by historians living at a later date.

—Richard Evans, *In Defense of History*, 1999

In the beginning was the past. There really was a "then." The past consisted of events, people, natural surroundings, and the landscape. In the distant past, time was measured in seasons and by the cyclic alternation of day and night, light and darkness. In most cultures, time was cyclic and repetitive, rather than linear. There was cosmos but no history. Most humans in the past lived lives of "ceaseless repetition of gestures initiated by others."[1] Replication, not invention, was the norm. They imitated celestial archetypes in rituals of eternal recurrence, repeating acts of gods or heroes, abolishing history and time. Events were meaningless except as periodic ceremonies of regeneration or repetition of primal events of creation, such as the great battle between the Babylonian god Marduk and the sea monster Tiamat. There was no real sense of history.

The *past* is not *history*. The past may be lost without a trace. Or it may be remembered or continually reinvented or imagined as story. The past may be absent or present as a reasonably true account or as useful fiction.

In the case of the Trobriand Islands people of the Pacific, their language had no tenses. They simply did not understand the meaning of past, present, and future. While they certainly *had* a history, their understanding of it differed from that of other cultures

Our senses—the smells, tastes, sounds, and sights—and our memories remind us of the past. We remember, and sometimes reinvent, the past that we do not forget. We remember things that happened in sequence, before or after, but rarely at any particular time. Material things in the present remind us of the past: leaking poison gas canisters from the two world wars in France and Germany; the DNA of disinterred bodies; fossils; ancient pollen; old photographs; bones. I once encountered dried bloodstains of the Russian revolutionary leader Leon Trotsky (1879–1940) on top of some of his papers in a Harvard University archive, vivid evidence of the past, if not exactly history. (History reminded me that he was killed by an ice ax blow to the head while hunched over his desk editing his papers in Mexico.) We remember now, but it happened then. The past existed once and is not invalidated by our approximate, incorrect, or disappearing memories of that past now, in the present. Perhaps this is what President Abraham Lincoln (1809–1865) meant by our "mystic chords of memory." There really was a past. We even may remember some of it. We may suppress or forget other parts of it.

Historians and other people often use the past to sanction present structures of authority, religious or secular. But alternative histories may also justify overthrowing that same authority. Genealogy legitimates monarchy and nobility or provides a guarantee of future salvation (for the Mormons, or Church of Jesus Christ Latter-day Saints). Marxist history legitimates revolution, not capitalist authority, as the final and inevitable product of history. The past may be used to explain the present and predict the future. But however the past is used and altered in the present, it was once there and then.[2] We seek its traces in the evidence we find in the present.

The past is intimately connected with *time*, a mysterious idea that we measure metaphorically in terms of space (a long or a short time). Early on, people developed calendars to help them keep track of past, present, and future time. Calendars are based on the motions of the natural world (sun, moon, stars, earth) and on a beginning of time (birth of a hero, founding of a religion or a nation, creation of the world, etc.). They contain both cyclic (hours, days, weeks, months, years) and linear (sequential years) elements. Cultures keep track of calendar time in many different systems. But calendars are a cross-cultural measure of past time. The Mayans measured time in terms of days, years, and *katuns* (7,200 days, or about twenty years). Mayan time was both linear and cyclic, so that knowledge of recurrent patterns of events gave power and authority to the priests and wise men and women who understood the past. One historian of calendar time defines time as "interconnected hoops rolling up a great hill of progress."[3] Western time (like Chinese time) is linear. But for many different cultures, time was cyclic, a wheel and not an arrow, eternal recurrence and not linear progress.

We all have remembered pasts. I ask my students to give an accurate account of what they ate for breakfast. I then ask them to suggest various ways in which they might obtain *evidence* about that breakfast (eyewitness testimony, receipts, fragments found, etc.) that would prove that their account was true. The results can be messy. But so is history. For human history involves historians and their human subjects in our common fate, that is, in what the German philosopher Immanuel Kant (1724–1804) called the "crooked timber of humanity." Unlike scientists, historians resemble the objects of their all too human study of the past. We do not need to get bent out of shape by the fact that we are all crooked timber. We understand others in the past precisely because they too, like us, were human beings.

The past, then, is not history. The past and its traces provide the raw material of history. We might well have begun with the evidence, those traces of the past that are accessible to us now, in the present. But without the raw material of the past, there would be no evidence in the present, no story to tell, and no history to discover and construct. So we begin with the past and with the root word of history, *story*.

Notes

1. Mircea Eliade, *Cosmos and History: The Myth of the Eternal Return* (New York: Harper and Row, 1959), 5.

2. J.H. Plumb, *The Death of the Past* (Boston: Houghton Mifflin, 1970).

3. Anthony Aveni, *Empires of Time: Calendars, Clocks and Cultures* (New York: Basic Books, 1989), 332.

For Further Reading

On the idea of the past, see especially Mircea Eliade, *Cosmos and History: The Myth of the Eternal Return* (New York: Harper and Row, 1959). The historian J.H. Plumb explores the difference between past and history in *The Death of the Past* (Boston: Houghton Mifflin, 1970). On time, see Anthony Aveni, *Empires of Time: Calendars, Clocks and Cultures* (New York: Basic Books, 1989). See also, from an art history perspective, George Kubler, *The Shape of Time* (New Haven: Yale University Press, 1962), as well as G.J. Whitrow, *Time in History* (Oxford: Oxford University Press, 1988).

An interesting recent study of memory in relating past and history is Patrick H. Hutton, *History and the Art of Memory* (Hanover, NH: University Press of New England, 1993).

2

Story

The fascinating thing about telling stories is that they start with the end.

—Joyce Appleby, Lynn Hunt, and Margaret Jacob, *Telling the Truth about History*, 1994

In any war story, but especially a true one, it is difficult to separate what happened from what seemed to happen. . . . The angles and vision are skewed.

—Tim O'Brien, *The Things They Carried*, 1990

Once upon a time, as we say, human beings maintained their family and community, in part, by telling stories about the past. They still do. Stories were generally oral, not written. Stories often contained as much fiction as fact. The storyteller might also be a healer or a magician. Today, literary critics talk of narratives more than stories. But *story* and *narrative* form the same linked chains of tales about the past.

Story in any culture forms the basis of *myth*, where gods and humans interact in a way that explains the natural world. The Greek poet Homer (c. 8th c. B.C.E.) in the *Iliad* and *Odyssey*, and the Roman poet Virgil (70–19 B.C.E.) in his *Aeneid*, provide memorable examples of the impulse to write down stories from a world of oral folk tales as epic poems. (We are not even certain that Homer was a real person, rather than a compilation of oral accounts.) There are many stories and gods in the polytheist universe of ancient Greece and Rome. Myths keep the collective unconscious alive by telling stories of gods and humans interacting in love and war. Many Chinese myths and stories claim to predict the future. We often live by such stories, which are told and retold with variations over and over.

One particular Greek story associates history with women. Clio was one of nine daughters of Zeus, god of the heavens, and Mnemosyne, goddess of memory. In time, Clio took on the role of the "proclaimer" of the past, or the muse of history. She ultimately became the patron of all historians. In the West, the story of history as a discipline begins with the Greek goddess Clio.

A story generally exhibits a plot that develops from a beginning through a middle section to an end. Think of this triad as past, present, and future. Good stories may or may not end happily ever after, but they end. The Hebrew Scriptures and the New Testament are examples of oral traditions become written stories in which God is the main stage director and narrator of human events, keeping the Hebrews to their covenant and promising salvation to Christians at the end of time, and in eternity beyond death. God speaks and makes promises. God hears and accepts sacrifices.

Stories exist to entertain, to moralize, to teach us about life. The *Iliad* glorifies war and exemplifies the Hellenic code of the hero. The *Aeneid* tells of the genealogy of empire and the transfer of that empire from Troy to Rome. The Florentine poet Dante and his Renaissance townsman, Boccaccio, were great storytellers who drew on the rich traditions of both pagans and Christians to portray the divine and human comedies. The Arthurian legends of late medieval France and England told stories of knights and ladies, magic and the quest for the Holy Grail. The Renaissance writer Christine de Pizan told stories about her imagined and liberated City of Ladies, unhindered by patriarchs. The Grimm brothers collected and reinvented German fairy tales. The British writer Katherine Mansfield (1888–1923) and the Russian Anton Chekhov (1860–1914) helped make the short story a modern art form. Stories persist as part of our culture.

"I am always at a loss to know how much to believe of my own stories," said American writer Washington Irving (1783–1859) in his *Tales of a Traveler* (1824). Stories normally contain more elements of fiction than are allowed historians.

History was originally an attempt to tell a true story, then to get the facts straight, to explain and even analyze the past. But in recent years the line between story and explanation, literature and history, has blurred. Some postmodern literary critics consider all the past a text and historians merely tellers of a relatively meaningful (or meaningless) story that they construct from textual fragments found. Texts are not necessarily fictions, of course. But our most important stories, especially stories about ourselves, may also be true or at least grounded in truth. Historians remain doggedly concerned with approximating the truth about the past on the basis of available evidence. Yet historians recognize, as they always have, their own present situation and inclinations. Recognizing their limitations, historians still want to tell true stories, not make up a fictional past. They want to figure out what probably happened, not what we might imagine happened.

Stories are like instructions for the craft of history. They narrate the step-by-step process of construction in sequence. But stories do not give us the raw materials unless they are true, nor the tools for construction. They are a useful beginning, and we should know them before we settle down to work.

We are, to paraphrase Aristotle, storytelling animals. But, as the contemporary writer of Vietnam War stories, Tim O'Brien, reminds us, stories blur the line between truth and fiction. Stories are normally fictional. They do not necessarily intend to tell the truth about the past. Truth and fiction may at times seem indistinguishable. *Story* is the root word for *history*. But stories about the past are not yet history, because they are not necessarily true. What, then, do we really mean by the word *history*?

For Further Reading

Story and history are closely related. My favorite analysis of the relationship is Norman Maclean, *Young Men and Fire* (Chicago: University of Chicago Press, 1992). Maclean tells his story of trying to discover and reconstruct the history of smoke jumpers killed in a fire that blew up in Montana in August 1949. The writer Tim O'Brien explores the similarities and differences between story and history regarding the Vietnam War in his *The Things They Carried: A Work of Fiction* (New York: Penguin, 1990).

3

History

The Register of Knowledge of Fact is called History.

—Thomas Hobbes, 1651

History is philosophy teaching by example.

—Bolingbroke, 1735

Historical research is a process of discovery and construction. The historian investigates what happened in the past by *researching the available evidence* in order to establish the facts and the chronology of events. This evidence may include written records, archives, manuscripts, maps, and documents, but also unwritten evidence—photographs, paintings, coins, records, tapes, videos, computer hard drives, and so on. The garbage of the past is everywhere. But from the very beginning, the historian must select and distinguish what is important and significant from what is unimportant and ephemeral.

History aspires to construct and tell true stories about the discovered past. Of course, truth about the past remains elusive and approximate. We can never be certain that we have understood the past correctly. But historians always *seek the truth* about the past insofar as that is possible. Truth is that never quite attainable straight line that is never precisely straight. As craftsmen, historians construct their story on the basis of evidence by selecting and arranging the facts (or ideas, values, or artifacts) in a chronological sequence that has a beginning, middle,

11

and end. Where the story begins and ends is a matter of interpretation, as well as discovery. In this process, past facts become present statements of fact, narrated after the fact by the historian.

In addition, history seeks to understand and explain past events by interpreting their meaning. The historian seeks to *discover* order and structure in the chaos and messiness of the past. The historian also *constructs* order and structure by creating a narrative or an argument, based on verifiable evidence. Historians know they live in a present where bias and interpretation of the past abound. They understand their own bias. Yet they try to be objective. In addition to telling a story, *they develop a persuasive argument* on the basis of the evidence, an argument that they believe is reasonable and accurate. They write about context, as well as text. They identify causes that will help *explain* how or why events happened the way they did. They seek *understanding* and *empathy* with individuals in another time and place. They persist in asking questions about the past: Why and how did events happen? What caused an event? Which individuals play important roles? And *what is the meaning* of the events studied, in terms of both past and present?

Why have I italicized some selected words and passages above? Because I think they are very important in understanding history.

Most histories began as *chronicles* or narratives of wars by men who had fought in those wars—the two Greek generals, Herodotus (485–425 B.C.E.) on the Persian Wars and Thucydides (460–400 B.C.E.) on the Peloponnesian Wars, for example. These early historians tried to narrate the story of events that actually happened. They tried to get the *facts* straight. They made explicit the evidence and sources for their statements of fact. They tried to be objective, even when they invented or imagined some of the evidence according to what others told them. They accepted some wild stories on faith and made up speeches they never heard in person. In Thucydides's account of public speeches in ancient Greece, for example, he made up what he "thought the situation demanded."

"History is the witness that testifies to the passing of times; it illuminates reality, vitalizes memory, provides guidance in daily life, and brings us tidings of antiquity. The first law for the histo-

rian is that he shall never dare utter an untruth. The second is that
he shall suppress nothing that is true. Moreover, there shall be no
suspicion of partiality in his writings, or of malice."

—Cicero (106–43 B.C.E.)

The Greeks invented history by trying to tell true stories about the
past. But history was often more *cyclic* than *linear*, going nowhere. In
contrast to the Greeks, the Hebrews made history meaningful and linear by making it *monotheistic*. The Hebrew Scriptures comprised a
series of stories that told of God's covenant with the people of Abraham
and Israel, his chosen people who promised to obey God's command-
ments and laws. God spoke to his people through burning bushes or at
sacrifices. Historical time was linear, not cyclical, beginning with the
creation of the world (Genesis) and ending with the coming of the
Messiah. In between lay nomadic wandering and endless suffering for
the Israelites. Prophets predicted the coming Messiah and a river cross-
ing to the land of milk and honey. One God gave *meaning* to the terror,
the wandering, and the suffering of history.

Christian history was also monotheistic and linear but added a *central sacred event* between the beginning and end of history, namely, the
appearance of Jesus Christ as the Son of God. Christians replaced Jews
as the chosen people in the New Testament, fulfilling the promise of a
coming Messiah. History began with the Garden of Eden and the creation of the world and with Adam and Eve's big mistake, original sin.
Free will could be dangerous. At the end of history, Christ would come
again to judge the quick and the dead after a final battle between the
forces of Christ and Antichrist, God and Satan. History would have a
meaningful end in which Christians would find eternal life and salvation from sin in Heaven, or else eternal death in Hell.

Christian history in the Middle Ages was often a *chronicle*, a listing
of wars, kings, queens, baptisms, plagues, and marriages. Chronicle
meant *chronology*, a listing in order in time of important events. But
monks also wrote and copied down Christian accounts of historical
events. Behind events stood only one cause—the will of an omniscient
and omnipresent God. History was moral drama, a story of God's judgment and a battle between God and Satan for the control of human
souls, a battle between good and evil. Medieval histories are full of the

stories of good men and bad, saintly women and wicked hags, chivalry and perfidy. "History records good things of good men," wrote the Venerable Bede (673–735) in the eighth century, and "evil of wicked men." Bede used multiple sources and cross-checked them; he also believed that what a bishop said about saintly bodies that allegedly did not decay simply had to be true because of divine authority.[1] The bishop on God's authority knew right from wrong, and truth from heresy. *Moral judgment* was a crucial element in medieval history, where God was omniscient, omnipotent, and omnipresent.

Medieval Christian history was above all *dualist*. History was a battle between two forces—God and Satan, light and darkness, body and soul, Heaven and Hell. St. Augustine (354–430) portrayed history as a story of the City of God and the City of Man. But some medieval history after around 1100 was also *triadic*. Purgatory became a third place between Heaven and Hell. The twelfth-century monk Joachim of Fiore developed a scheme of history that divided all time into three ages that reflected the Father, the Son, and the Holy Spirit. The scheme sounded a lot like past, present, and future. And Joachite thinking became the archetype for later tripartite schemes of the nineteenth century, including the thesis-antithesis-synthesis logic of the Prussian philosopher Georg Wilhelm Friedrich Hegel (1770–1831) and the feudalism-capitalism-socialism stages of history described by the radical social thinker Karl Marx (1818–1883). The line between medieval and modern history was more continuous, and less sharp, than the moderns initially pretended.

Medieval history also meant *genealogy*, a family history that justified ruling authority through a line of royalty, or nobility through marriage and descent. Virgil's great account of the genealogy of Rome, how Aeneas fled burning Troy to found Rome (despite an affair with Dido, shipwrecks, and a descent to the underworld), provided a model of a genealogical epic of a founding father. Virgil also hoped to please his contemporary patron, Emperor Caesar Augustus. In the late Middle Ages, an entire profession of genealogists emerged to chart, and sometimes to forge, lines of noble descent.

The words *history* and *historian* only appeared in English around 1500. A *historian*, as distinct from a chronicler or annalist, tried to provide a true, written narrative of past events, not simply a year-by-year listing. Historians began to distinguish between primary (direct) and secondary (secondhand) sources. But most historians were simply people who wrote history as a hobby. Griots, shamans, and storytellers were the first professional historians. But historians did not organize themselves professionally as a group until the end of the nineteenth century.

A *primary source* is a document, image, or artifact that provides us with evidence about the past. A *secondary source* is a book, film, article, or museum that displays primary sources selectively in order to interpret the past.

The Renaissance and the Enlightenment gradually made human beings and human actions more central to human history. History became in part the study of change over time, more accurate, more systematic, more focused on human, rather than divine, activities. In time, the practice of history divided into two varieties—call them *positivist* and *idealist*—which viewed history as science or as art.

Science by the eighteenth century gave history two quite different sets of metaphors to employ in the language of narrative and explanation, *mechanical* and *organic*. Mechanical metaphors involved words like *force, mass, energy, inertia, revolution, rise,* and *fall*. These words came largely from physics and Newtonian mechanics. (Russian revolutionary Leon Trotsky used to talk about the locomotive of history racing down the tracks of time.) Organic metaphors involved words like *birth, life, death, growth, culture, evolution,* and *decay*. (The German philosopher Johann Gottfried Herder [1744–1803], whose ideas on culture and peoples influenced later romantic and nationalist historians, distinguished between mechanical *civilization* and organic *culture*, a distinction of enormous importance to later German and Russian thought.) Historians today employ both mechanical and organic metaphors, often quite unconsciously. Watch out for them in your reading!

After the Enlightenment, some historians claimed to be practicing a kind of science, seeking to sift and weigh evidence critically, to test the validity of sources by cross-examination, and to classify and organize evidence in the manner of a geologist or paleontologist. Some critics called them *positivists*. The German historian Leopold von Ranke (1795–1886) epitomized this impulse when he offered seminars to university students in Germany on historical method. Ranke claimed that history sought to explain, to understand, as well as narrate, the past "as it really was." To do this, historians needed to empathize with people of another time and place, to put themselves in their place, and to get the facts straight. Some claimed that history would "speak for itself." Others claimed that history, like science, could establish laws of human behavior over time. History, proclaimed the British historian J.B. Bury around 1900, was "herself simply a science, no less and no more."[2]

Other historians and philosophers of history—notably Wilhelm Dilthey (1833–1911), Benedetto Croce (1866–1952), and Robin G. Collingwood (1889–1943)—became *idealists*. That is, they emphasized that history was really contemporary, here in the present, and autobiographical, about the historian in the present as much as about the historian's topic in the past. They focused on what people thought, felt, and imagined as much as on what they did. They showed that ideas and ideologies were causes of actions in the past. Some became intellectual historians, historians of ideas.

The idealist historian sought to understand the past by getting imaginatively inside the minds of individuals in the past. Collingwood in his book *The Idea of History* (1943) distinguished between the inside and outside of events. The outside of events meant simply actions, bodies in motions, what people actually did. The inside of events meant the thoughts, values, and ideas of the human actors who made history. The purpose of history was empathy and understanding of others. By studying the mental world of the past, historians sought to inhabit the minds of their subjects, knowing that this requires imagination inspired by evidence. The historian could then reenact past actions the way those who performed them were thought to act.

Positivist ("scientific") historians claim that history provides a scientific explanation of past actions and events. Some philosophers argue that such explanations presume a "covering law." For example, to explain the 1917 Russian Revolution in terms of two main causes—the disastrous effects of World War I and the presence of an organized conspiratorial political party, the Bolsheviks, ready to seize power—is to presume a law something like this: "Whenever a society experiences defeat and destruction in war and contains a political party organized to overthrow the government, a revolution will result." Thus, positivists believe that explanation is equivalent to prediction. The statement "x and y caused z" is equivalent to the statement: "If x and y, then z." Explanation implies a power of prediction that most historians would reject, but may sometimes imply. Historians generalize, but rarely claim to be discovering a law.

Most historians simply accept that history is part science and part art. They can only try to explain the causes of past events. They work to understand the intentions and motives of historical personages, but can be certain about neither. Both scientific explanation and imaginative reconstruction remain elusive goals. The point is simply to try to explain and understand past events by testing a general hypothesis against particular and specific evidence. The result must always be contingent and subject to revision.

Historiography involves the study of the writing of history. It describes historical arguments, theories, and interpretations over time, how schools of thought on particular events change over time—like history.

For example, historians continually argue about, debate, and revise our understanding of the causes of the American Civil War. They usually distinguish between causes that were necessary and those that were sufficient to cause a civil war. Necessary causes include sectional differences between North and South, the existence of slavery as an institution, the moral and political critique of slavery, and the dispute over the tariff. Given the existence of these necessary causes, then other causes were in the end sufficient to lead to a civil war—the Kansas–Nebraska Act of 1854, the election of Abraham Lincoln as president in 1860, or the federal decision to resupply Fort Sumter in Charleston Harbor in 1861, and the southern firing on the fort. Without the necessary causes, the sufficient causes would probably not have been sufficient. With them, they produced war and endless suffering—and monumental changes—in both North and South. (See the longer example of causation and the Civil War in the toolbox section of this book.) Historians rarely make their causal models explicit. But they often assume them.

Causation is like an explosion. Necessary causes are like dynamite, plutonium, or hydrogen—that is, the fuel. Sufficient causes are like the fuse, match, implosion lenses, or atomic trigger—that is, the ignition device. Ignition causes explosion—but only because the fuel is present.

After the middle of the nineteenth century, the idealistic impulse of some historians shifted to a form of history that sought to find the ultimate meaning of historical events within, rather than outside, history, in human action rather than divine intervention, in large patterns and forces operating over time. Recent critics have dubbed this trend *metahistory*. If historians are generally trying to understand the subtleties and complexities of many things, metahistorians are trying to understand THE ONE BIG THING that gives meaning to history.

Notes

1. Venerable Bede, *Ecclesiastical History of the English People* (London: Penguin Books, 1990), 41–43.
2. Fritz J. Stern, *The Varieties of History: From Voltaire to the Present* (New York: William Collins, 1956), 223.

For Further Reading

A good selection of philosophical writings on history is Fritz J. Stern, *The Varieties of History: From Voltaire to the Present,* (New York: William Collins, 1956). See also Patrick Gardiner, *Theories of History* (New York: Free Press, 1959).

A classic positivist view by a leader of the *Annales* school is Marc Bloch, *The Historian's Craft* (New York: Alfred A. Knopf, 1953). A more recent exposition is Fernand Braudel, *On History* (Chicago: University of Chicago Press, 1980). On the history of the positivist dream about scientific history, see Peter Novick, *That Noble Dream: The "Objectivity Question" and the American Historical Profession* (New York: Cambridge University Press, 1988).

For the idealist counterpoint, see Robin G. Collingwood, *The Idea of History* (New York: Oxford University Press, 1943). A more specialized, but brilliant, essay on history, free will, and determinism is Isaiah Berlin, *The Hedgehog and the Fox: An Essay on Tolstoy's View of History* (New York: Mentor, 1957).

On historians as a breed, see J.H. Hexter, *On Historians* (Cambridge: Harvard University Press, 1979), and *The History Primer* (New York: Basic Books, 1971).

A fascinating collection of essays on history as mystery is Robin W. Winks, ed., *The Historian as Detective* (New York: Harper and Row, 1968). In the same vein of historical fun, see David Hackett Fischer, *Historians' Fallacies: Toward a Logic of Historical Thought* (New York: Harper and Row, 1970).

4

Metahistory

The history of the world is none other than the progress of the consciousness of freedom.

—G.W.F. Hegel

The history of all hitherto existing societies is the history of class struggle.

—Karl Marx

Metahistory seeks to find one all-encompassing meaning in history.[1] Metahistorians and system builders believe that history has its own meaning internally. Historians can thus discover meaningful laws and patterns in history over time. The intellectual revolutions initiated by the British naturalist Charles Darwin (1809–1882) and the German philosopher Friedrich Nietzsche (1844–1900) made God extraneous to history, if not entirely dead. Judaism and Christianity provide powerful divine metahistories. But after 1850, the idea of God's will and design acting in history gave way to ideas of the survival of the fittest species by natural selection, and to the will to power of the Overman. But Darwinian natural selection and Nietzschean escape from the prison of history were only two varieties of *historicism*, the view that history has its own meaning and pattern and laws. Historians merely had to discover those meanings, patterns, and laws.

Metahistory emphasizes ideal patterns and regularities. Some metahistorians leaned toward science and system. The so-called positivists, especially the French philosopher Auguste Comte (1798–1857), believed that the study of history was, or could become, a science. Comte too believed in historical stages. The past was not only meaningful but law-like (the iron law of wages, the law of business cycles, laws of the rise and fall of civilizations, and so on). In part, metahistory derived from medieval and early modern natural law theory, divine in origin but knowable through human reason. History was often repetitive (for example, as tragedy and farce) and therefore knowable and discoverable. In this sense, metahistory extended and transformed the Christian view of history as meaningful and linear. But history was secular, not sacred. History, not God, contained the great design of the universe.

The German philosopher Hegel was a metahistorian. He replaced God with the Absolute and saw history as an evolving process of progress toward freedom. All quests for truth were dialectical in that they began by stating a thesis, then developed its antithesis, or opposite, and finally resolved them in a synthesis. Karl Marx studied Hegel's method and became a materialist, seeing material possessions as the basis of culture and society. Marx considered all history the history of class struggle and oppression—the thesis—leading to revolution—the antithesis—and the seizure of political and economic power by the working class (proletariat) from the capitalist class that owned the means of production (bourgeoisie)—the synthesis. (Ironically, the term *revolution*, borrowed from physics, initially implied not linear development, but cyclic return, the recovery of rights lost.) In England, the so-called Whig view of history extended the Enlightenment project to see all history as continuing rational progress toward a happier future of the greatest good for the greatest number based on encyclopedic knowledge of the world. History meant progress, for individuals and for societies. Life was simply getting better and better.

Other thinkers claimed that all history was biography. They emphasized the individual lives of great men and women who "made history" in the past—Henry VIII, Frederick the Great, Joan of Arc, Elizabeth I. Still others traced the rise of peoples and nations—Treitschke and Droysen in Prussia, Macaulay and Trevelyan in England, Soloviev and Kliuchevsky in Russia, Guizot and Michelet in France, Parkman and Bancroft in the United States—and gave nationalist meaning to history. Nations were like individuals. They were born, they developed, and they perished. The nation-state was the primary object of historical study. History also became a means of defining and asserting national identity. Politically, nationalism, liberalism, and socialism informed nineteenth-century metahistory after the revolutions of 1848. So historians naturally turned to studies of nations, individuals, and social classes. Liberalism and socialism created master narratives of progress and revolutionary emancipation.

History and memory are closely connected. We cannot afford amnesia if we are to function in the present. The memory hole (a term coined by British writer George Orwell [1903–1950] for eliminating inconvenient history) can destroy both truth and identity, as well as function.

By 1900, metahistory turned to the ideological and irrational in history. Sigmund Freud (1856–1939) and Carl Jung (1875–1961) opened up the subterranean world of the irrational and the unconscious to psychoanalysis and psychohistory. All history was the history of neurosis resulting from mankind's perpetual struggle to repress unconscious urges, longings, and desires, notably those of sex. Jung interpreted history in terms of persistent archetypes. Dreams became evidence for analysis of the psyche. "The riddle of history," the Freudian philosopher Norman O. Brown wrote later, "is not in Reason but in Desire; not in labor but in love."[2] Psychoanalysis offered a way out of history, freedom from the burdens of a repressed past, the sublimated instincts of Eros and Thanatos, love and death.

Metahistory also turned more speculative. In the wake of World War I, Oswald Spengler (1880–1936) wrote his massive *Decline of the West* (which he dictated on a machine), describing the organic laws of the rise and fall of civilizations and of what he called Apollonian, Magian, and Faustian cultures within Western civilization. He produced two almost unreadable volumes. Arnold Toynbee followed with his massive study of the rise and fall of civilizations according to rules of challenge and response to crises. Both looked for law-like explanations for the collapse of the West after a terrible war. Likewise, after World War II, theologian Reinhold Niebuhr (1892–1971) articulated a modern Protestant vision of history by reinstating God as sovereign maker of history and its "one story," full of irony and paradox. Niebuhr again placed meaning outside of history and in religion.

Unfortunately, some metahistory also nurtured totalitarianism. Metahistory provided the underpinnings of two monstrous dictatorships of the twentieth century in Europe: Nazi Germany and Soviet Russia. German leader Adolf Hitler and Soviet leader Joseph Stalin based their two police states on race and class, anti-Semitism and Marxism, respectively. Racist thinkers in Germany explored the history of so-called Aryan race and predicted future Aryan domination over non-Aryan races. Marxist thinkers in Russia reduced all history to formulas of class struggle. The ideologies of anti-Semitism and class struggle dominated all thought and reduced individuals to pawns in an evil chess game. Individuals went to the gas chamber or the gulag simply because they stood in the way of history.

Nazis and Marxists also rewrote, or altered, history to suit the party line, not the truth. The Aryan race and the working class became the collective heroes of a deadly new kind of official history. Historians criticized the official approach at their peril. (Subscribers to the *Great Soviet Encyclopedia* were once surprised to receive in the mail a razor blade and an article on "berylium" to replace the inconvenient entry on "Beria" after police chief Lavrenty Beria was shot following Stalin's death in 1953. Beria became an unperson—literally written out of history.) Historians had to make their work conform to the established orthodoxies of the party line, Nazi or Communist. If they did not, they became—as Soviet leader Nikita Khrushchev once put it—"dangerous people." The party line defined truth.

In the case of the great French medievalist and historian Marc Bloch (1886–1944), who helped found the journal *Annales* and reinvent history as a social science, metahistory literally killed history. The Gestapo tortured and murdered Bloch for his work with the French Resistance during World War II. Millions of others lost their lives because they failed to conform to the standards of metahistory or dared to criticize that metahistory as defined by Nazi or Soviet leaders.

But metahistory not only created ideologies. It subverted them as well. Marx, Darwin, and Freud were great demystifiers of history. They concluded that history was not what it appeared to be, simply the story of individuals making choices over time. History was a mystery to be revealed. They had revealed that mystery. They were realists, not romantics. History was really a struggle determined by a single force—a struggle to eliminate class inequities and injustices, a struggle to enable the fittest species to survive, or a struggle to repress or sublimate sexual desires by creating civilization. Individuals were not independent entities, but members of groups. Groups made history. Those in power wrote history. To explain history as it really was meant to strip away the repressive language of ruling elites and other groups in power and to discover and reveal the real and true meaning, the metahistory, underneath that deceptive discourse.

Twentieth-century metahistorians took a "linguistic turn" (following the philosophers), reducing history to a kind of language game. Postmodernism, in addition to deconstructing the language of power, created its own language to replace the organic and mechanical metaphors of the past—*body*, *other*, *colonial*, *imperial*, *space*, *discourse*, *narrative*, *empowerment*, and *text*, to name a few choice words. By claiming that history was merely a form of text, the postmodernists annoyed most historians with their relativism, skepticism, and language games. They also contributed valuable insights into the importance of language in historical studies and in the craft of history itself.

A recent, and more benign, example of metahistory involves evolutionary biology and genetics. Some call it *memetics*. By this theory, cultures evolve in a process of natural selection that favors the most durable *memes* (cultural genes, or viruses). A *meme* is a cultural unit such as an idea, a value, or a fashion fad. Some catch on immediately. Some become quickly extinct. History develops organically and has a pattern. DNA determines the outcome of history as cultural evolution. Cultural evolution follows Darwinian logic. History has a core pattern that can be studied scientifically—the epidemiology of core ideas and values. One speculative thinker thus concludes that "both organic and human history involve the playing of ever-more-numerous, ever-larger, and ever-more-elaborate non-zero-sum [winning does not necessarily mean losing, and vice versa] games."[3]

Another example of metahistory is the current concept of "Jihad versus McWorld," which interprets contemporary history as a struggle between the forces of tribal nationalism and holy war on one side, and the forces of global integration and international corporations on the other. The deadly attack on New York's World Trade Center and on the Pentagon on September 11, 2001, epitomized that struggle.

In any event, metahistory, which began as a philosophical effort to fill the metaphysical void left by the death of God in the nineteenth century, became speculative. At its best, metahistory helped historians and readers see the larger meaning of history. At its worst, metahistory provided the ideological justification for totalitarianism. Politicians distorted history to justify nationalism, genocide, and ethnic cleansing. We are not yet done with the great simplifiers who have used history to serve their own ideological ends.

In the meantime, historians sought to analyze, rather than simply narrate, the story of the past without making any grand assumptions about meaning. History became less positivist, more empirical, and more probabilistic, more pragmatic in its approach. Historians and metahistorians went their separate ways. "To analyze a complex phenomenon," as one contemporary historian observes, "a single theory, however rich and multivariate, will seldom suffice. Complex events usually have multiple causes."[4] The age of metahistory and great speculative theories about the past seems to be behind us. But there will always be those who claim to understand the one big thing that gives meaning to history.

Notes

1. Hayden White used the term *metahistory* in his book *Metahistory: The Historical Imagination in Nineteenth-century Europe* (Baltimore: Johns Hopkins University Press, 1973). White defines history as "a verbal structure in the form of a narrative prose discourse" and "a specifically Western prejudice by which the presumed superiority of modern, industrial society can be retroactively substantiated" (ix, 2). Few historians accept White's view.

2. Norman O. Brown, *Life against Death* (Middletown, CT: Wesleyan University Press, 1957), 16.

3. Robert Wright, *Nonzero: The Logic of Human Destiny* (New York: Vintage, 2000), 6.

4. Victoria E. Bonnell, *Roots of Rebellion: Workers' Politics and Organizations in St. Petersburg and Moscow, 1900–1914* (Berkeley: University of California Press, 1983), 17.

For Further Reading

The place to start is with a massive study rejected by most historians, Hayden White's *Metahistory: The Historical Imagination in Nineteenth-*

century Europe (Baltimore: Johns Hopkins University Press, 1973). The classic liberal Whig interpretation is the subject of Herbert Butterfield, *The Whig Interpretation of History* (London: Penguin Books, 1931). A modern Christian metahistory essay is Nikolai Berdyaev, *The Meaning of History* (Cleveland: Meridian, 1968 [1936]). Arnold Toynbee portrays history as the challenge and response of great civilizations in *A Study of History* (New York: Oxford University Press, 1957).

On history as narrative, text, and virtual reality, see Hayden White, *The Content of the Form: Narrative Discourse and Historical Representation* (Baltimore: Johns Hopkins University Press, 1987).

Paul Costello summarizes the work of twentieth-century metahistorians (H.G. Wells, Spengler, Toynbee, Pitrim Sorokin, Lewis Mumford, and William McNeill) in his *World Historians and Their Goals: Twentieth-century Answers to Modernism* (DeKalb: Northern Illinois University Press, 1993).

On the new cultural evolution approach to history, see Susan Blackmore, *The Meme Machine* (New York: Oxford University Press, 1999).

5

Antihistory

The unhistorical and the superhistorical are the natural antidotes against the overpowering of life by history; they are the cures of the historical disease.

—Friedrich Nietzsche, "The Use and Abuse of History," 1874

The only grounds for preferring one [historical interpretation] over another are moral or aesthetic ones.

—Hayden White, *The Content of the Form,* 1987

As long as there has been history, there have been those who opposed or denied history. The English poet Matthew Arnold (1822–1888) wrote of "that huge Mississippi of falsehood called history." Stephen Daedelus in Irish novelist James Joyce's *Portrait of the Artist as a Young Man* called history "a nightmare from which I am trying to awake." History is a basically rational enterprise. Thus, the currents of irrationality that flooded Europe in the twentieth century also inundated the historical profession. The central threats to those who sought to tell the truth about history were excessive idealism and relativism.

Historians are notorious for asking questions: Who? What? When? Where? How? Why? Question-framing is crucial to the historian's craft. Without a significant question, one is unlikely to get a significant answer.

Idealism had its roots in the philosophy of Bishop George Berkeley (1685–1753) and Immanuel Kant, the notion that ideas (like Platonic forms) had reality and that history was essentially the history of ideas. All history was intellectual history, the history of thought. History was not science, but art. Artists would paint whatever picture they chose. Nietzsche argued that future "supermen" would substitute their own ideas for religion to manipulate the herd of humanity. The point was not to remember the past, but to forget it, and liberate our true selves. History was simply an idea, not a reality. And ideas were only true relative to the person who thought those ideas.

There is certainly nothing wrong with emphasizing ideas, understanding, and empathy in doing history. But to emphasize the idea at the expense of the evidence is inappropriate. So if there were many historians, then there were many ideas of history. Historical truth was no longer absolute, but relative to the historian. Every man was his own historian, as American historian Carl Becker (1873–1945) put it around 1930. Relativism meant that there was simply no way to choose which of two or more competing histories of the same events was preferable. There was no absolute truth, simply relative truths that pragmatically worked for different historians. The facts and the meaning were impossible to agree upon. Interpretation was all.

In some cases, historicism gave way to scepticism and postmodernism. History, in the opinion of the anti-Semitic automobile manufacturer Henry Ford, was bunk. If all interpretations of history were equally valid, or meaningless, why not choose the one that worked? Ford believed in the spurious anti-Semitic forgery known as the *Protocols of the Elders of Zion*, which explained the history of the modern world in terms of a Jewish conspiracy, and he disseminated these views widely in the 1920s. (See section 13.4, "Forgeries and Facsimiles," in the toolbox.) Some idealists and relativists turned to fascism. Benedetto Croce admired Italian fascist dictator Benito Mussolini (1883–1945). The German philosopher Martin Heidegger (1889–1976) became a member of the Nazi party. The Belgian literary "deconstructionist" Paul De Man (1919–1983) wrote for Nazi journals during World War II. The French philosopher Jean Paul Sartre (1905–1980) went along with Stalinism in the Soviet Union. And after the war, existentialism produced a literature of despair in which history was a meaningless struggle for existence, Sisyphus endlessly rolling his rock up the hill, the stranger wandering in the void. Despair bred nihilism and relativism. History seemed a tale of sound and fury, signifying nothing, as Shakespeare and William Faulkner put it.

In writing history, you should be true to the facts, report your sources accurately, write in the past tense, avoid "I," be as objective as possible, make passive sentences active, and choose your words carefully. Don't be vague, wordy, pretentious, or gender-specific. Organize well. Be brief.

Fortunately, historians generally tended to resist totalitarianism, not to collaborate with it. If they could not resist, they sometimes refused to go along with the party line and "wrote for the drawer," waiting until a freer time to publish their findings.

During the Cold War, censorship and secrecy became the enemies of history. Classification of secret documents in closed archives made crucial evidence off limits to historians not cleared to see such information. Government control of information proliferated. Under the Official Secrets Act, "weeders" routinely eliminated inconvenient documents and files in British archives. (Not everything in the Public Record Office, as one bureaucrat put it, was open to the public.) Whole archives were closed or disappeared into shredders. History fell down the "memory hole," as British writer George Orwell described it. In the Soviet Union, not only people, but history in general, was purged, cleansed, revised to suit the party line. Historians were afraid to publish their findings for fear of arrest or worse. Only in the United States did the Freedom of Information Act (1966) finally come to the aid of historians and reopen secret archives to public scrutiny. Even then—and even today—bureaucrats have found ways to subvert or delay the release of previously classified information.

I once discovered the secret 1950 "confession" of British atomic spy Klaus Fuchs in the Truman Presidential Library. The German-born Fuchs worked at Los Alamos, New Mexico, the supersecret center of the Manhattan Project to build the atomic bomb during World War II. Fuchs passed information on nuclear weapons to the Soviet Union. The document recording his confession to British intelligence interrogators was classified "top secret" in Britain, but was internal to an unclassified memorandum to President Truman in the United States. I published the confession in my biography of Fuchs in the early 1980s. Shortly afterward the American document was reclassified. Such is the wilderness of mirrors of classification and secrecy.

The most recent example of antihistory is the idea that fiction and nonfiction are identical. Some postmodern thinkers consider all history a form of text or narrative. The past does not exist. Reality does not exist. Truth does not exist. Time does not exist. The facts do not exist. History is a story constructed (not discovered) by the historian. One story is as good as another. No story is falsifiable. Take your pick:

- The Holocaust never happened.
- A massive conspiracy killed President John F. Kennedy in 1963.
- Alger Hiss was completely innocent of all charges.
- Ancient Greek civilization came from black Africa because Aristotle stole his ideas from Africans in the library at Alexandria, Egypt.
- A Blair Witch project existed in Burkettsville, Maryland.
- Japanese soldiers did not torture, rape, and kill hundreds of thousands of people in Nanking, China, in 1937–1938.
- The biographer Edmund Morris grew up with Ronald Reagan in the 1920s.
- The Druids discovered America.

These are all erroneous statements of fact. There is no evidence to support any of them. There is much evidence to contradict them. But many people believe them. Who wants to choose between competing lies?

So the difference between fact and faction is central to doing history. Yet some literary critics proclaim all history a text or a useful fiction. History is all interpretation. Historians make up details that suit their narrative. Biographers (such as Edmund Morris) insert themselves into the biography of another person as if they had known him or her. Films perpetuate completely discredited historical theories about events (director Oliver Stone based his film *JFK* on a discredited report on the Kennedy assassination [see section 13.6]). Historians even write books on what might have happened, rather than what did happen, confusing prophecy and vivid imagination with history.[1]

The most notorious example of antihistory is historical denial. Historical denial asserts that a well-known event never really happened or that a well-known person never existed. In accordance with relativism, those who deny history assert that all views of history are equally valid, just a bit different. They claim that their denial is just as valid as any other historical account. Thus the Holocaust, a series of events and actions that killed 6 million Jews and other "subhumans" during World War II, either happened or did not happen. Take your pick. The "revisionists" deny that it happened at all. People usually deny that past events happened for present political reasons. They ignore the normal rules of science, reason, and logic. They distort, or take out of context, selected facts that suit their opinion or argument. They ignore all evidence that contradicts their claim. They exaggerate claims based on one piece of evidence, not many. They substitute bias for open-mindedness toward the past. They cite discredited sources that agree with their point of view. Historical denial is *not* historical revision, a perfectly acceptable way of rethinking the past. Denial is pseudohistory.

A single fact neither proves nor disproves a historical argument. History is grounded in multiple facts and sources, streams of evidence pointing to a single conclusion. Denying one fact proves nothing.

Historians themselves are not immune to the virus of extreme relativism and useful fiction. Historian Simon Schama joins the language game of antihistory by introducing into his histories "purely imagined fiction" and "purely fictitious dialogues" along with a true account of events. Thus Schama transforms history into a partly fictional work of the imagination "worked up from my own understanding of the sources as to how such a scene might have taken place."[2] (See the example of Schama's fictitious British soldier's account of scaling the cliffs of Quebec in section 13.2.)

Of course, once we begin mixing history and fiction, we may well invalidate the history as a whole. If one fact is made up, why not the next? And the next? And the next? However brilliant and well written, antihistory is speculation or fiction, not history.

Notes

1. For example, Robert Cowley, ed., *What If? The World's Foremost Military Historians Imagine What Might Have Been* (New York: Putnam, 1999). These essays imagine "likely outcomes had history gone differently"—Hitler deciding not to attack the Soviet Union in 1941, Atlantic storms hitting the Normandy beachheads for one additional day in June 1944, the Confederacy winning the Civil War, Nazi Germany occupying Great Britain, and so forth.

2. Simon Schama, *Dead Certainties* (New York: Vintage, 1991), 327. Schama admits that the observations of one of General Wolfe's soldiers prior to the Battle of Quebec are "pure inventions based, however, on what the documents suggest," but denies that he would ever "scorn the boundary between fact and fiction," that is, history (322).

For Further Reading

On the denial of history, see especially Deborah Lipstadt, *Denying the Holocaust: The Growing Assault on Truth and Memory* (New York: Free Press, 1993), and more recently Michael Shermer and Alex Grobman, *Denying History: Who Says the Holocaust Never Happened and Why Do They Say It?* (Berkeley: University of California Press, 2000).

Postmodernism has had a greater impact on literary criticism than on philosophy or history. For a favorably inclined collection of essays, see Keith Jenkins, *The Postmodern History Reader* (London: Routledge, 1997). A more hostile response to postmodernism is Keith Windschuttle, *The Killing of History: How a Discipline Is Being Murdered by Literary Critics and Social Criticism* (Paddington, Australia: Macleay, 1996). The title says it all. A more balanced account is in Mark Poster, *Cultural History and Postmodernity: Disciplinary Readings and Challenges* (New York: Columbia University Press, 1997).

6

The Present

All history is contemporary history.

—Benedetto Croce

What I offer you here is in part my invention, but held tightly in check by the voices of the past.

—Natalie Zemon Davis, *The Return of Martin Guerre,* 1983

Present and past interact in the mind of the historian. But when does the past end and the present begin? Perhaps the past ends with one's own birth year or, perhaps, yesterday. Agreement is impossible. There is no clear way to distinguish contemporary history from past history. Besides, history has always involved the historian in the present describing a past that once existed but now needs to be reconstructed. History has even been defined as the "simultaneous perception of difference and similarity between past and present."[1] What can the past teach us about the present? How does our present inform our view of the past?

Some idealist historians claim that all history is present, or contemporary. History is a product of the life and mind of the historian here and now. Some positivists claim that history is a weak science of description, if not prediction, which can approximate the truth about a past that really existed. But history is a large tent under which sit many historians of different interests, from intellectual history to material culture, from cultural history to economic history. There is room for all, except perhaps for those who wish to tear down the tent.

Legitimate *revision* of history involves filling a gap in the literature, changing an accepted interpretation by presenting new facts, or rearranging old facts to provide new interpretation of the past.

Professional historians, of course, are a community of practitioners. They are craftsmen and craftswomen. They continue to research and write history essentially the way they always have. Many remain blissfully ignorant of, and uninterested in, the theoretical dogfights that rage around them. They simply go on doing history.

Historical interpretations meanwhile undergo periodic revision. New schools of history (sometimes fads, or fashions) develop to fill gaps in the literature or to open up new fields—economic history, quantitative history, psychohistory, postcolonial studies, cultural studies, and so on. Historians continue to employ useful methods from other disciplines, notably sociology, economics, linguistics, and anthropology. Historical journals and on-line historical Web sites proliferate. Teams of historians revise the conventional wisdom of old topics. Biography and film bring history alive in new and exciting ways, conveying history to a broad audience untouched by the average scholarly monograph.

In recent years, historians have also become less elitist and more inclusive. The men's club that was history now is an equal opportunity, even affirmative action, employer. Historians now include more women, minorities, and gays than ever before. Many have their own organizations and special interest groups. History has expanded its topics to include women's history, African-American history, labor history, the history of the body, the insane, and the differently abled. Likewise, historians borrow liberally from other disciplines, notably anthropology, linguistics, and sociology. Virtually everyone is now the subject of historical study. Anyone can become a historian. The workshop and craft of history are open to all.

Historians study continuity and change over time. They look for long-term trends, as well as short-term turning points. They study

what did not change, as well as what did change, social structures
as well as events.

In the twentieth century, the school of French historians centered
around the journal *Annales* had an enormous impact on researching
and writing history. These historians sought to achieve more scientific
history by examining very long periods of time (*longue durée*), a worldwide geographic perspective in space (*l'histoire totale*), the mental world
(*mentalités*) of people in the past, and any and all evidence that might
bear on the structure of society—weather reports, linguistic terms and
phrases, aerial photographs, crop production, prices, and geography,
for example. (In one case, a historian used archival statistics on the
number of candles burned in particular French churches in the Middle
Ages to look at regional variations in religious fervor!)

The past cannot speak except through the sources after interroga-
tion. But historians of recent events can interview subjects who
are still alive and willing to speak. Oral interviews are a significant historical source, because the historian can cross-examine a
witness to events who is living, not dead.

The *Annales* historians and their successors have tried to return history
to its scientific origins and to shift historical study away from politics
and foreign policy to society and culture, including material culture.
While they do not ignore political events, they focus on social history.
They are partly responsible for the general shift in historical studies
toward social and global history, and away from narrative to analysis.
What matters to them is not the history of events, but the structure of
society that changes very slowly over time.

Present-day historians develop a number of useful skills that will
help them in virtually any future career or activity:

- Research—finding, selecting, and weighing evidence
- Judgment—distinguishing good evidence and arguments from bad
- Persuasive argument
- Good, close reading of written texts

- Good, concise writing of logical narratives and analysis
- Question-framing that is significant
- Simple and direct presentation of a case study.

One historian, David Potter, characterized all historians as either *lumpers* or *splitters*, people who put things together or take them apart. More likely, historians begin with some simple assumptions that tend to lump things together, then encounter the incredible complexity and diversity of the past, then try to find their way through to a new way to lump things together that provides a better explanation than has been provided to date. Put in another way, historians encounter data, frame a hypothesis, and modify that hypothesis if they encounter new data that require such modification. In any case, historians develop useful skills of investigation and expression.

Living in the present, rather than the past, also raises the question of *bias*. How can the historian overcome present opinions and personal predilections to write a reasonably objective account of the past? Contrary to the notion that all history is autobiography, historians need to understand and empathize with people and cultures of other times and places. They are less likely to study themselves than the other, the stranger, the kind of person they never will be because they lived in another time and place. Current identity politics tends to steer historians toward topics of race, class, and gender and to characterize individuals in terms of a group or social class. Historians can never overcome present politics entirely. But they should make the attempt. And they should make their own bias explicit for the reader as part of their history.

Today, historians continue to break new ground in our knowledge of the past. They may fill a gap by studying an unknown topic or individual. They may synthesize existing sources that concern a sprawling, interdisciplinary topic like the history of New York City. They may rearrange knowledge by studying what happened in a particular year, say, 1831. They may study new and "forbidden" topics such as the history of contraception. They may reinterpret a familiar subject such as Abraham Lincoln in a new way, perhaps emphasizing his religious views. They may reexamine a famous primary source, such as the Declaration of Independence. They may look at the lives of ordinary people "from below" in extraordinary times, such as Stalin's purges of the 1930s. They may launch a team effort to have many historians reexamine a well-known event, such as the American Civil War. Or they may turn to a study of the language or discourse of the past to understand political culture and folkways.[2]

History has always been partly a product of the present historian, as well as the past. Historians choose what to research and write about, when and where to begin and end their story, and how to construct a true narrative. They do not, or should not, invent useful and dramatic fictions or leave out and suppress inconvenient evidence in the archives. They should use their tools wisely, and maintain them in good condition, like any other craftsmen.

Notes

1. Jacques Barzun, *From Dawn to Decadence: Five Hundred Years of Western Cultural Life* (New York: HarperCollins, 2000), 47.
2. See Maria Diedrich, *Love Across the Color Lines: Ottilie Assing and Frederick Douglass* (New York: Hill and Wang, 1999); Edwin G. Burrows and Mike Wallace, *Gotham: A History of New York City to 1898* (New York: Oxford University Press, 1999); Louis P. Masur, *1831: Year of Eclipse* (New York: Hill and Wang, 2001); Andrea Tone, *Devices and Desires: A History of Contraceptives in America* (New York: Hill and Wang, 2001); Allen C. Guelzo, *Abraham Lincoln: Redeemer President* (Grand Rapids: Eerdmans, 1999); Pauline Maier, *American Scripture: Making the Declaration of Independence* (New York: Alfred A. Knopf, 1997); Sheila Fitzpatrick, *Everyday Stalinism: Ordinary Life in Extraordinary Times: Soviet Russia in the 1930s* (New York: Oxford University Press, 1999); Gabor S. Borritt, ed., *Why the Civil War Came* (New York: Oxford University Press, 1996); Kenneth Cmiel, *Democratic Eloquence: The Fight over Popular Speech in Nineteenth-century America* (Berkeley: University of California Press, 1990).

For Further Reading

The journal *History and Theory: Studies in the Philosophy of History* is an excellent place to start discovering how philosophers, critics, and historians think about history today. A good overview of historical thinking by a practicing historian is Richard Evans, *In Defense of History* (New York: W.W. Norton, 1999). See also Joyce Appleby, Lynn Hunt, and Margaret Jacob, *Telling the Truth about History* (New York: W.W. Norton, 1994). Philosophically inclined students will appreciate William H. Dray, *Philosophy of History*, 2d ed. (Englewood Cliffs, NJ: Prentice Hall, 1993). A good history of twentieth-century trends in historiography is George Iggers, *Historiography in the Twentieth Century: From Scientific Objectivity to the Postmodern Challenge* (Middletown, CT: Wesleyan University Press, 1997).

For a good case study on how history can be entangled in present politics and painful memories of the living, see Edward T. Linenthal and Tom Engelhardt, eds., *History Wars: The* Enola Gay *and Other Battles for the American Past* (New York: Henry Holt, 1996).

On history as a male enterprise, see the history of women in the profession by Bonnie G. Smith, *The Gender of History: Men, Women, and the Practice of History* (Cambridge, MA: Harvard University Press, 1998). Also, Joan Scott, *Gender and the Politics of History* (New York: Columbia University Press, 1989).

7

The Future

Historians do not make very good futurists. The so-called futurists of the European avant-garde before World War I imagined a coming world of racing cars more beautiful than ancient Greek sculpture. (Maybe they were right, given the popularity of NASCAR.) They disdained everyone over age thirty. Many of them died violently in the mud and trenches of the Great War. Historians failed to predict the rise of Nazi Germany in the 1930s or the fall of the Soviet Union in 1991. But history is not a craft of prediction, like meteorology. So we cannot predict for certain that the future of history itself holds promise. Historians disagree in that regard.

Although history is not predictive, it can offer some useful perspectives and counsel prudence for decision makers in the present. History provides marvelous critical tools for puncturing inflated analogies— for example, between two different centuries, the Vietnam War and the rise of Hitler, the origins of very different wars. (Bismarck's comment that the Balkans were not worth the bones of a Prussian soldier is currently popular. So is the analogy between the Maginot Line and the Star Wars antimissile system, or between the medieval assassins of Central Asia and present-day terrorists.) Decision makers who have read history widely and deeply may well have better virtual historical experience for making decisions than someone quite ignorant of the past. But they may also be tempted to use the expression "history shows" to precede an inaccurate, uninformed, or misleading statement.

History cannot predict the future. Unlike science, history does not study laws of nature but specific events in the past. History cannot run controlled experiments. Fortunately, we are not condemned to repeat history, but free to make the best of it.

History will continue to survive in the natural selection process that creates and destroys modes of knowing. History as a species of knowledge is deeply rooted in the human condition, our need for true stories about the past. Particular forms of history, however, have become, and will continue to become, extinct. Hagiography (laudatory lives of saints) has pretty much disappeared, except in the biographies of dictators like Saddam Hussein and Idi Amin, or the campaign biographies of American presidential candidates, or the pop memoirs of sports heroes and rock stars. (Come to think of it, maybe hagiography is still alive and well. . .) We do have our modern heroes—Michael Jordan, Elvis Presley, Mother Teresa, Martin Luther King, Britney Spears. But historians no longer assume the primacy of individuals, or even of politics, policy, and diplomacy. Intellectual history has given way, at least temporarily, to social history and cultural studies. Even postmodernism has probably had its day, relatively speaking.

The field of evolutionary biology has provided historians with a new word, the *meme*. Memes are like genomes or perhaps computer viruses. They are replicators. They convey information and send messages that determine which memes will survive in the meme pool and which will not. Memes may be ideas, slogans, tunes, poems, or clothing fashions. Imitation means survival. Otherwise they will become extinct, like the concept of the ether, or the Absolute, or Great Men, or the Edsel. Genomes survive, but computer viruses can be eliminated. In this model, history is a meme that will survive the struggle for existence. History has enormous powers of both replication and adaptation. Despite the assault of postmodernism, history as a discipline is here to stay.[1]

History will probably remain partly art and partly science, construction and discovery. Historians cannot simply paint whatever picture they imagine. Nor can they run controlled experiments in the present to verify hypotheses about the past. Rather, they continue to construct products for the marketplace of historically curious readers, using the materials of the past, the blueprint of story and narrative, supplies of evidence, and the rules of the trade. Readers (and reviewers) of history in the end will determine which history survives, becomes popular, is relegated to the scholarly journals, or disappears.

A source may be both primary and secondary, depending on its use. For example, Joyce Appleby's *Liberalism and Republicanism in the Historical Imagination* (1992) is a secondary source about liberal and republican thought. But it is also a primary source about Joyce Appleby, women historians, and American historians in the late twentieth century. Our purpose partly determines whether a source is primary, secondary, or both.

Thus, the historical profession will continue to adapt and change. Historians will work within existing paradigms or establish new ones. Students of history will not be clones of their mentors, but voyagers on a new and exciting journey of their own. We know only that they will go to times and spaces that we have not yet seen. They will employ new methods, study new topics, and revise our view of what we thought we knew.

The Internet offers exciting new opportunities for historians. It provides a global data base, powerful search engines, access to the card catalogs of distant libraries (I often pay a virtual visit to Harvard, Dartmouth, or the Library of Congress before heading north for the summer), chat rooms, e-mail, and the opportunity to submit and edit a journal article entirely on-line. Yet there is also a downside to the Internet. There is often no peer review. Garbage and erroneous information abound. There is no editing or cross-checking, no guarantee of accuracy. The Internet is a powerful tool for research.[2] But it is also misleading and incomplete. Historians tend to use it only as an ancillary tool or a starting point for research.

There is ample evidence that history is alive and well. The documentary films of Ken Burns testify to a deep American need to rediscover the past through visual and musical historical materials. The History Book Club has wide readership. Millions read history for fun and pleasure. Companies like History Associates Incorporated (with which I have had the good fortune to be affiliated) provide litigation support, archival services, and historical research and writing for corporate and government clients.[3] Historical controversies over issues such as the arsenic-laden hair of Napoleon, the bones and DNA of dead czars and presidents, and the Holocaust become front-page news. Daniel Goldhagen's book *Hitler's Willing Executioners: Ordinary Germans and the Holocaust* (New York: Knopf, 1996) created a furor in Germany and the United States by arguing that ordinary Germans, not just Hitler and the Nazis, participated actively in killing Jews.[4] Historical preservation groups in virtually every community fight to save and restore old buildings, to collect historical artifacts from families, to publish anniversary accounts of towns and regions. Companies research and write history for corporate and government clients. Television has a channel devoted to nothing but history.

We also have people apologizing for past historical injustices. Everywhere political and religious leaders apologize (and sometimes pay reparations) for past crimes against humanity—the Crusades, Galileo's imprisonment, slavery, the American internment of Japanese-Americans during World War II, Stalin's purges, and Hitler's Holocaust. In this way, history becomes public mythology. That mythology too is subject to revision. Apologizing for history has become a postmodern growth industry of late capitalism. If history offends, apologize. And bring on the lawyers!

History exists both in the knowable past and in the present mind of the historian. History is neither scientific fact, nor relativist fiction. Historians both discover and describe the past through narrative and persuasive argument, or interpretation. They are detectives and writers, craftsmen, not scientists or artists. In explaining the course of a past event—how and why it happened—historians provide an interpretation that is provisional and temporary. History is continually tested and revised by other historians. History involves revision, not denial, of statements of fact about the past, based on new facts or new interpretations of old facts, not on present politics. The community of historians produces converging lines of evidence that create a testable hypothesis about the past. Historians then test, examine, and rethink that hypothesis in the complex craft that is history. On occasion, they may even rethink the paradigm of history itself.

Like a lawyer, the historian builds a case upon the historical evidence. Like a detective, the historian seeks clues to solve a mystery. Like an artist, the historian paints a picture that expresses a personal vision. Like a scientist, the historian frames and tests falsifiable hypotheses against the data. But in the end, the workshop of the historian perhaps most resembles the workshop of the craftsman. The historian aims to make history a true and readable account of the past limited only by the materials, the plans, and the design. That account must ultimately be grounded in fact, not fiction.

As long as human beings survive to tell stories and ask questions about the past, history will survive. History is not just narrative and text. Nor is it likely to become, well, just history. History is a durable and venerable branch of knowledge in a liberal arts curriculum. But it is also a craft whose knowledge and tools will serve students well in any occupation or career over the changing course of their lifetime. Most students will not become professional historians. But they will use the historian's tools, consciously or unconsciously, every day of their lives. And they will read history for enjoyment and understanding. Remember that. And write it down.

Notes

1. On memes (a word coined by geneticist Richard Dawkins in 1976), see especially Richard Brodie, *The Virus of the Mind: The New Science of the Meme* (Seattle: Integral Press, 2001).

2. A good history Web site is http://www.ukans.edu/history/VL/, which has numerous links to other historical and archival sites.

3. See, for example, Philip L. Cantelon, *The History of MCI: The Early Years, 1968–1988* (Dallas: Heritage Press, 1993); Richard Hewlett, *Jesse Ball du Pont* (Gainesville: University of Florida Press, 1992); Joan Zenzen, *Battling for Manassas: The Fifty-year Preservation Struggle at Manassas Battlefield Park* (State College: Pennsylvania State University Press, 1998).

4. See Geoff Eley, *The "Goldhagen Effect": History, Memory, Nazism—Facing the German Past* (Ann Arbor: University of Michigan Press, 2001), for a historical study of a historical controversy.

For Further Reading

On the limited uses of history for decision makers, see Richard E. Neustadt and Ernest R. May, *Thinking in Time: The Uses of History for Decision-Makers* (New York: Macmillan, Free Press, 1985). On history as analogous to film and photography, see Siegfried Kracauer, *History: The Last Things Before the Last* (New York: Oxford University Press, 1969).

For an excellent guide to the Internet for historians, see Dennis A. Trinkle and Scott A. Merriman, eds., *The History Highway 3.0* (Armonk, NY: M.E. Sharpe, 2002).

Part II

The Tools of History

8

Doing History: An Overview

The best way to understand history is to try to do some history yourself. The following examples should help you to choose a good research topic, begin your reading, take good notes, and write a good final paper. In time, you will discover other tools and hone them for yourself.

8.1 Choosing a Good Paper Topic

Choosing a good paper topic is a challenge and an important first tool in researching and writing history. How big should the topic be? How small? Can you do the topic justice in the short period you have to research and write it? Here are some friendly questions to ask yourself when choosing a paper topic:

1. Will this topic maintain my interest and fascination over a long period of time?
2. Do I have the necessary background in reading and course work to undertake research about this topic?
3. Is this a topic about which other historians have written (historiography) rather than simply a topic of personal interest to me?
4. Is this topic feasible in the sense that there are primary sources (documents, correspondence, autobiographies, records, etc.) available to me for research purposes?
5. Is the topic really historical (say, before I was born), or is it so contemporary that historians have not yet explored it?

6. Is the scope of the topic too big and broad (modern Russia), too small and narrow (Lenin's speech at the Finland Station, April 1917), or just about right (the response of the Bolsheviks to the Provisional Government in 1917)?
7. Does the topic present a significant question that can be reasonably answered in this case?
8. Will this paper contribute anything original to the historical discussion? Fill a gap in the literature? Or at least take sides in an ongoing historical debate?
9. Will I have fun researching and writing about this topic? Will it make a good story, as well as a convincing argument?
10. Can I explain to my niece, nephew, parent, or friend what the topic is and why it should be of any interest to them?

Task: Write a brief account of how and why you actually chose your topic for a recent history paper. Which of these criteria did you satisfy? Which did you not satisfy?

8.2 Reading History

Reading is another critical tool in doing history. You should read as much history as you can. Reading history is different from reading novels, or poetry, or essays, or scientific articles in a technical journal. The volume of work on any historical topic is normally so large that it could take the better part of a lifetime to read through it with any care. What should you read? How should you read works of history? What techniques can help you know when and how to skim, or read carefully, or selectively?

Historians rarely start at the beginning of a book and read through to the end. This kind of reading is pleasurable. But the sheer volume of sources makes it impossible for historians to read everything completely. Rather, they approach each source with specific questions or interests in mind that automatically limit the amount of material that will be relevant to them.

Historians will often start with the index of a book to see what entries might be of interest to them and related to their topic or question. They may then move on to the bibliography, which tells them how thorough and relevant the book's "data base" is to their own research.

Is the book up to date on historiography? Has the author consulted all the relevant sources? A glance at the introduction and acknowledgements can also be useful. Who has assisted in the research and writing of the book? Who has read the manuscript prior to publication? A book's bibliography then becomes part of the historians' virtual bibliography they are constructing as they read more and more about a topic.

Historians also learn to skim a book briefly to see what its scope and quality offer to them. The table of contents and a look at relevant sections as indicated in the bibliography should suffice. They may find a brief section or two of some value and decide to copy it for later use. But you should avoid copying in the early stages of your reading until you have a clear question and focus in mind.

As you read history, you should simultaneously be thinking about your topic and how the reading relates to it. This will help you read selectively and quickly. You should also get in the habit of rereading. Historians often consult a work more than once. Each time they reread that work they may see a new dimension helpful to them. Rereading primary sources from the archives can be especially important.

This morning I began to think about this selection. What might appeal to students? What would be a good example of historical reading? With that purpose in mind, I chose a book to reread, Franklin Ford's *Political Murder: From Tyrannicide to Terrorism* (Cambridge, MA: Harvard University Press, 1985). I thought the example of President Lincoln's assassination by the actor John Wilkes Booth on April 14, 1865, in Ford's Theater in Washington, D.C., might be interesting to students. I used the index to find an entry on Lincoln on pages 350–53. I decided to copy a brief paragraph (350) after I skimmed those pages. The example follows:

> "Booth's devotion to the Confederacy appears to have been sincere enough, albeit grounded in emotion and melodramatically expressed. In the months following Gettysburg, and still more after the President's reelection in 1864, as Grant's and Sherman's armies applied ever more relentless pressure upon an exhausted South, Booth's anti-Union sentiments became correspondingly stronger. His hatred of Lincoln in particular drew added virulence from much that a biased and selective

> observer could pick up even in the North from an environment poi-
> soned by the seemingly endless war, with its casualties, draft riots, short-
> ages, and disappointments. In October 1864, just a month before Booth
> appeared for the last time on stage with his brothers, Edwin and Junius,
> Jr., playing the part of Mark Antony in *Julius Caesar* before an audi-
> ence of two thousand at New York's Winter Garden Theatre, he began
> a series of trips to Montreal for clandestine meetings with Confederate
> representatives in Canada. There, in collaboration with desperate South-
> ern agents, he conceived in its original form his plan to help reverse the
> tide of Union victories."

This selection intrigued me partly because of the passage about Booth's
trip to Montreal to meet Confederate agents. There are several recent
books on the topic of the Confederate secret service and the Lincoln
assassination. I wanted to recall more about Booth's trip to Montreal
and his meetings there. The whole question of Confederate complicity
in Booth's plan to kill Lincoln came back to mind. This reading re-
kindled my interest in the Lincoln assassination in a new way, aside
from choosing a selection for this book. I began reading with one purpose in mind and discovered another purpose in the process. One reading almost always leads to many more readings. I needed to read more
after rereading this passage.

On the need to reread history, consider the judgment of an editor
about the high quality of historian John Erickson's history of the Red
Army titled *The Soviet High Command: A Military–Political History*
(New York: St. Martin's, 1962), and his other books: "They really merit
three or four readings. In fact, the fifth or sixth reading will produce
new judgments on the part of a reader. In other words, his books have
to be studied" (*New York Times*, March 19, 2002, A25). There is no
short cut to reading history well. Rereading a text carefully is as important a tool for doing history as reading it for the first time.

Task: Photocopy a page from a history book you have read recently.
Mark the passages which (1) provide information, (2) seem worth quot-
ing in your own work, and (3) provide interpretation of the subject.
Remember that defacing books is not a good idea. Taking good notes
on your reading is better.

8.3 Taking Notes

Taking notes carefully and keeping them in order are essential tools in all historical research. How can you learn to take good notes? Good question! Some famous writers and historians have found themselves accused of plagiarism because they failed to take careful notes or to check those notes against the sources before publishing their own work (see section 10.4).

Taking good notes begins with the historian's principle of *selectivity*. You cannot write everything down that is germane to your topic and your research. Copying everything down is as hopeless a task as trying to remember everything without taking notes at all. So learn to select what is important from what is merely interesting or informative as you read and take notes on that reading.

Learn to *paraphrase* (say in different words) or *summarize* (say more briefly) the words of another author in order to capture their meaning in brief without borrowing their language. A paraphrase normally uses about the same number of your words to convey the words of another person. A summary normally reduces the words of another to fewer words of your own.

Remember to put quotation marks around any phrase, sentence, or paragraph that is not your own words, but those of another author. If you do not do this, you may well return to your notes in a few days, weeks, months, or years and come to believe that you yourself wrote words that, in fact, originated with another person. Failing to use quotation marks properly while taking notes can easily lead to plagiarism later.

When copying down the words of another, do not edit or correct the prose. You can later indicate any errors or misspellings by putting the correct entry in [brackets] in your later paraphrase, summary, or citation.

Keep a full citation (author's complete name, title, place of publication, publisher, and year of publication) for all books. The same goes for articles and archives. Keep each citation on a separate card in a file that can later serve as your bibliography. Then use a shorthand note (Smith, 277) to refer briefly to the source and page number on every note card you use that is taken from that source.

Keep notes on separate note cards. (I prefer four-by-six-inch cards for convenience, since three-by-five-inch cards don't seem to hold enough words, and five-by-eight-inch cards can waste a lot of space and trees unless you have a lot of words to put on them.) You can then use these cards to organize and reorganize your material as you go along. A good card file in the end can lead easily to an outline or first draft of your paper. And you can always reorder the cards as you modify your topic or your argument.

Task: Take notes on this section of *The Historian's Toolbox* by listing the main points about good note-taking. Which points seem familiar? Which are new?

8.4 How to Write a Good History Paper

Writing clear and concise prose in ordinary language is a fundamental tool of any historian. How exactly can you learn to write a good history paper, or a good paper in any class? Individuals surely vary in their writing and research abilities. But the following suggestions may help you find your own voice and skills as you do history:

1. Choose an interesting topic that you think is important. Get excited about it. Read quickly and widely. The topic should not be too large (the Civil War), nor too small (the rifle pits at Fort Fischer in 1864), but just right (Fort Fischer during the Civil War and the naval blockade of the South by the North). The topic should be feasible: there should be sufficient primary and secondary sources on the topic, but not so many that you could not possibly get through them in the time allotted. (On primary and secondary sources, see chapter 9.) If the topic is significant, there should be some secondary sources by other historians on the same topic.

2. Ask a good question that you may be able to answer. (How effective was the Union naval blockade of Fort Fischer during the Civil War?) The question might ask how or why an event happened (causation, explanation). It might ask what the consequences were of a particular event. It might discuss the intellectual origins of a particular idea. It might ask what the cultural context of an event was. It might ask whether or not an individual was responsible for a certain act. It might ask about the social history of a political event or quantify broad trends in a society at a particular time.

3. Research the topic and compile a bibliography of primary and secondary sources you have consulted or will consult. Search and research the topic. Read through books and articles more than once as you learn more. Identify the key primary sources that tell directly about the topic, as well as the secondary sources that argue about issues or questions related to the topic. Use one four-by-six note card for each item, with a brief comment or annotation on its usefulness. Include or exclude items from the bibliography as you research the topic. Consult your college or local library and use the Web to search the catalogs of other libraries. Expand your bibliography as you look through the bibliographies at the back of your secondary sources. Remember to write down complete citations for each entry.

4. Take notes carefully and selectively as you read. Be neither a human Xerox machine nor a master of total recall. Learn to be selective about what you write down. Make sure that you put quotation marks around the words of others so you can cite them accurately and fairly later on. Use a system of note cards whose order can be reshuffled and rearranged at will. If helpful, use colored or tabbed cards to separate the file topically. Indicate dates on each card for putting in chronological order. Indicate on each card in abbreviated form your source, which you have in full on a separate card. As you progress, you should take fewer and more significant notes. Accuracy and thoroughness will pay off later.

5. Investigate the historiography of your topic, that is, how historians' interpretations of it have developed and changed. Who has written what on the topic? When? What are the major issues and arguments about? How have they framed the topic and the question, or questions? How has each secondary source used and taken account of (or taken issue with) previous sources? What different schools of thought on the topic/question exist? Read quickly and widely at first, then more selectively and carefully again . . . and again. Think about reframing your initial question (and even topic) as you learn more.

6. Develop your own argument about the topic that answers a question. Your argument should make a good point and support that point with evidence. Does your argument "fill a gap"

in the existing literature on the topic by providing new facts? Does it support an existing interpretation or argument that you think is more convincing than other interpretations? Does your argument represent a new interpretation of the topic? Does it employ a new method to look at an old topic? In any event, in this critical stage you situate your topic and your argument within existing historiography. Don't forget that you need to tell an interesting story (narrative), in addition to arguing a case, or solving a puzzle, or answering a question. At its root, history is story.

7. Write a complete outline of your paper. The outline is the skeleton of a story and argument you will flesh out in your paper. A sentence outline is best (each entry is a complete sentence) because it forces you to think about each point you are making as you develop the paper. Use the outline to define the topic once again, to reframe the question, and to structure the answer in a logical and persuasive way. A page or two should do it. Don't forget to give the paper a title—this challenges you to think about what to tell your mother you are doing and even to persuade her to read the paper. Reread the outline several times. Does it make sense? Should it be reordered before you start writing?

8. Write a first draft of your paper. Then consider writing a second and third (computers are wonderful for editing and moving paragraphs). Get all your ideas and information down on paper, even if the draft seems too long—you can always go back and shorten it, as you probably should. Brevity counts. So does logic. Start writing anywhere—beginning, middle, end—that you feel most knowledgeable and comfortable. You can rewrite, abbreviate, and reorganize later. Let your ideas flow. Strive for clarity, precision, and accessibility even at this stage—your readers (audience) have probably not been spending the last week, or month, or year studying this topic. Think about the readers and how they might respond to every word you write. Be empathetic—put yourself in the reader's place.

9. Write a final draft. Make the language of the paper sing. Reduce the earlier drafts by writing more concisely and less redundantly. Use short words and short sentences. Start each

paragraph with a strong lead sentence. Avoid the passive voice (use "Kennedy defeated Nixon" rather than "Nixon was defeated by Kennedy"), split infinitives, jargon, ill-defined terms, long words, misplaced antecedents, and poor grammar. Use proper citation and style as indicated by the instructor, the department, or the publisher. Make everything consistent. Use footnotes (or parenthetical citations within the text) to cite your sources. Add a selective bibliography that identifies your major sources and the major secondary literature.

10. Proofread the entire paper from beginning to end at least once. Don't trust your computer's spellcheck program. Look up strange or apparently misspelled words in a dictionary. Fix grammatical and syntactical errors. Break up long sentences. Fix split infinitives. Check that the page numbers are in order. Is this a paper you are proud of? Would you want it published? Shared? You're all done? On time? Congratulations! You are a historian.

Task: Make a checklist of the above suggestions that you normally follow when writing a history paper. Which might you want to incorporate in your next paper that you had not considered? What other suggestions can you think of?

9

Sources and Evidence

History is, among other things, an argument based on sources and evidence that support that argument. Historians are not free to tell a story or make up an argument without supporting evidence. Evidence includes primary and secondary written sources (mainly documents) and nonwritten sources—maps, artifacts, images, quantitative data, and genetic evidence. The evidence of the sources is the raw material of history and the historian's most valuable tool. Historians should not argue or narrate beyond what the evidence demonstrates is the truth.

9.1 Primary and Secondary Sources

Primary and secondary sources are the crucial tools of the historian. A primary source is a document, image, or artifact that provides evidence about the past. It is an original document created contemporaneously with the event under discussion. A direct quote from such a document is classified as a primary source. A secondary source is a book, article, film, or museum that displays primary sources selectively in order to interpret the past. The two passages below related to the Wannsee Protocol provide a good example of the distinction between a primary and a secondary source. The Wannsee Protocol was the account written during World War II by Adolf Eichmann, who was present at a conference held on January 20, 1942, in the Berlin suburb of Wannsee to discuss the "final solution" of the "Jewish question." The original document, written in German, is in the Archives of the Foreign Office of the Federal Republic of Germany, and a translation is reprinted in A. Grobman, D. Landes, and S. Milton, eds., *Genocide: Critical Issues of the Holocaust* (Los Angeles: Simon Wiesenthal Center, 1983, 442–49). The first passage below is an excerpt from the Wannsee Protocol. It is a primary source. The second passage is an excerpt from Michael Shermer and Alex Grobman, *Denying History: Who Says the Holocaust Never Happened and Why Do They Say It?* (Berkeley: University of California Press, 2000). It is a secondary source, a book about the history of Holocaust denial.

Primary Source: The Wannsee Protocol (1942)

> Under appropriate direction the Jews are to be utilized for work in the East in an expedient manner in the course of the final solution. In large (labor) columns, with the sexes separated, Jews capable of work will be moved into these areas as they build roads, during which a large proportion will no doubt drop out through natural reduction.
>
> The remnant that eventually remains will require suitable treatment; because it will without doubt represent the most resistant part, it consists of a natural selection [*naturliche Auslese*] that could, on its release, become the germ-cell of a new Jewish revival. (Witness the experience of history.)

Secondary Source: Denying History: Who Says the Holocaust Never Happened and Why Do They Say It? (2000)

> The "evacuation of the Jews" Eichmann describes cannot mean simple deportation to live elsewhere, since the Nazis had already been deporting Jews to the east, and Eichmann indicates this was inadequate. Instead, he outlines a new solution. Shipment to the east will mean, for those who can work, work until death, and (as we know from other sources) for those who cannot work, immediate death. What about those who can work and do not succumb to death? *"The remnant that eventually remains will require suitable treatment."* Suitable treatment can only mean murder. Why? Eichmann explains that a natural selection (*naturliche Auslese*) in the Darwinian sense will make these Jews the most resistant (to death by exhaustion), meaning they will be the fittest—the youngest, healthiest, smartest, etc. Should this population of naturally selected Jews survive, they might (Eichmann fears) "become the germ-cell of a new Jewish revival." History, Eichmann points out, supports this theory of social Darwinism.

Illustration 9.1   **Wannsee Protocol, January 20, 1942**

L a n d	Zahl
A. Altreich	131.800
Ostmark	43.700
Ostgebiete	420.000
Generalgouvernement	2.284.000
Bialystok	400.000
Protektorat Böhmen und Mähren	74.200
Estland – judenfrei –	
Lettland	3.500
Litauen	34.000
Belgien	43.000
Dänemark	5.600
Frankreich / Besetztes Gebiet	165.000
Unbesetztes Gebiet	700.000
Griechenland	69.600
Niederlande	160.800
Norwegen	1.300
B. Bulgarien	48.000
England	330.000
Finnland	2.300
Irland	4.000
Italien einschl. Sardinien	58.000
Albanien	200
Kroatien	40.000
Portugal	3.000
Rumänien einschl. Bessarabien	342.000
Schweden	8.000
Schweiz	18.000
Serbien	10.000
Slowakei	88.000
Spanien	6.000
Türkei (europ. Teil)	55.500
Ungarn	742.600
UdSSR	5.000.000
Ukraine 2.994.684	
Weißrußland aus-	
schl. Bialystok 446.484	
Zusammen: über	11.000.000

How does a secondary source utilize a notorious primary source? The Wannsee Protocol of January 20, 1942, lists the number of Jews in various parts of Europe slated for the "final solution." *(House of the Wannsee Conference, Memorial and Educational Site: http://www.ghwk.de/Seite6.jpg)*

Summary

In sum, the Wannsee Protocol is a *primary source*. It provides a direct description of an event by a participant and eyewitness who wrote down what he heard and saw. The book *Denying History* is a *secondary source*, the work of two historians telling the story of Holocaust denial using documents such as the Wannsee Protocol. In the case shown above, we have a secondary source interpreting and commenting directly on a primary source.

   Task: Reread the secondary source selection. Which comments seem supported by the words in the primary source? Which comments seem speculative and go beyond what is demonstrated in the primary source?

9.2 Documents

The main type of primary source historians use is a document. A document is a written piece of evidence from the past. Historians use documents as the basis for putting together a narrative or analysis of past events. Documents provide historians with clues and information but must be used carefully and selectively.

A Revolutionary War Ancestor's Pension Application (1832)

My great-great-great-great-grandfather, Harris Chadwell (1746–1834) of Lynn, Massachusetts, was a soldier in the Continental Army during the American Revolution. He was part of a militia unit from Lynn, which joined the "minutemen" at Lexington and Concord in 1775. He in fact fired at British soldiers with his musket and then, fearing that he would be captured, threw his uniform shirt in a convenient pond and ran. In 1832, at the age of eighty-six, after telling (and undoubtedly improving) stories about his Revolutionary War exploits and adventures in local taverns for fifty years, he decided to apply for a pension offered by the U.S. government for surviving veterans of that war. This is a copy (or facsimile) of my ancestor's verification from the Commonwealth of Massachusetts that his name did indeed appear on a military list of Continental Army officers and soldiers in 1775. The original document of which this is a copy may be found in the National Archives in Washington, D.C. If you want to verify the

Illustration 9.2   **Military Pension Application of Harris Chadwell, Lynn Massachusetts, June 25, 1832**

A document is the basic tool of historical evidence: The Military Pension Application of my Revolutionary War ancestor, Harris Chadwell, of Lynn, Massachusetts, dated June 25, 1832. Chadwell, then eighty-six years old, had fought at the battles of Lexington and Concord in 1775, or at least taken a few shots at redcoats before throwing his uniform in a pond. What are some of the facts the document provides? (*National Archives*)

existence of this document, you could write (as I did) to National Archives and Records Administration, 7th and Pennsylvania Avenue NW, Washington, D.C. 20408.

This document could be used for several purposes: in a biography of my ancestor, Harris Chadwell; a Chadwell genealogy; a history of the battles at Concord and Lexington during the Revolutionary War; a history of the Continental Army; a history of the Lynn militia; a history of Revolutionary War pensions and pensioners; and so forth.

Did he get his pension? Other documents suggest that he did, but he died two years later, duly rewarded by his town and his country for what he may—and may not—have done during the war.

Task: List some other historical purposes or arguments for which this document might provide useful evidence. What does this document tell us? How reliable is it? Is there any reason to doubt it? Might there be errors in the document? What does the document leave out?

9.3 Maps

How can maps be historical tools? An old map used long ago would certainly constitute a primary source, providing direct evidence of how people saw the world at that time. But a later map would most likely constitute a *secondary source*, showing how a later historian wanted to construct or illustrate the past. We discover maps used in the past for various purposes, but we construct maps that help us explain that past.

Sebastian Munster's Map of the Americas, c. 1540

A sixteenth-century map of the Americas by a German scholar named Sebastian Munster provides an excellent and rare example of a historical map. Munster (1489–1552) was, together with Abraham Ortelius and Gerardus Mercator, one of the great cartographers of the age of discovery. He was also a mathematician, a professor of Hebrew, and (briefly) a monk. Munster's map is a woodcut originally published in his edition of Ptolemy's *Geographia* (Basel, 1540). Called "Die Nüw Welt," or "The New World," it was the best-known and most widely circulated map of the Americas of his day, the standard map until Ortelius's Americas map of 1570 appeared. Munster's map has many obvious mistakes. It incorrectly shows a northwest passage

64

Illustration 9.3   **Map of the Americas, c. 1540**

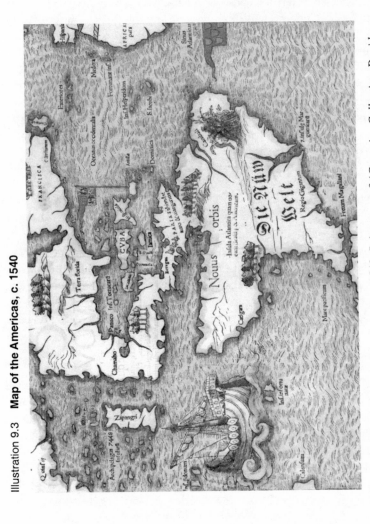

Sebastian Munster's map of the Americas, 1540. Is it accurate? (*Cumming Collection, Davidson College Library*)

to India and an inland sea, suggested by Verrazano's voyage of 1524, that nearly separates North America at the Outer Banks of North Carolina. This misconception made people think that they could easily find a route across North America to the wealthy Spice Islands in the East. Munster also catered to European fascination with "cannibals" by drawing them in what is now Brazil.

But Munster got a lot of things right. Florida, Cuba, and the general shape of the continents—despite their distortions—are easily recognizable. Munster was the first European mapmaker to show the recently discovered Western Hemisphere, the first to name the Pacific Ocean (*Mare Pacificum*), one of the first to depict Japan (*Zipangri*) on a map, and the first to show North and South America linked by land (Central America).

The Munster map is the oldest map in the William P. Cumming Map Collection at Davidson College in Davidson, North Carolina. The Cumming collection of forty-eight early maps offers the best set of maps of the American southeast in the world. For an introduction to the collection, see *The William P. Cumming Map Collection* (Davidson, NC: Davidson College, 1993). On the possibilities (often ignored) for historians to utilize maps in their research and writing, see Mark Monmonier, *Mapping It Out: Expository Cartography for the Humanities and Social Sciences* (Chicago: University of Chicago Press, 1993).

Ancient maps such as Munster's helped transform how Europeans envisioned their world, showing both its vast size and the existence of continents previously unknown to them. Though vastly different in subject, they are comparable in effect to contemporary images of distant solar systems, galaxies, and nebulae. These modern images help us picture the immensity of the universe much as Munster's map helped people picture the immensity of the planet. This sixteenth-century map is thus a key historical document that opens a window on people's knowledge and understanding of the world at a specific moment in time.

Task: Look closely at Munster's map. What other misconceptions can you see? What else looks correct? Compare it with a modern map of the Americas. How are they similar? How do they differ? What region did Munster portray most accurately? What does this reveal about the origins and goals of European exploration of the Americas? Why might Munster have put in the northwest passage? What does the map tell you about European conceptions and misconceptions about the New World?

9.4 Artifacts

An artifact is an object made by humans that is of anthropological or archaeological interest. How can old artifacts provide tools for studying the past? How do we interpret them? Do artifacts ever change our view of what happened? Where does history leave off and archaeology begin?

Digging Ancient Moscow

In recent decades, Russian archaeologists have engaged in constant excavations around the sprawling city of Moscow in hopes of learning more about the city's past. Tradition, based on an entry in the major document of old Russia, the so-called *Chronicle of Bygone Years*, dates the founding of the city in the year 1147. Thus, in 1997, the city celebrated its 850th anniversary with great pomp and circumstance, including even more intense archaeological digging. This digging yielded a trove of artifacts, including jewelry, shoes, ash and residue, and other items from ancient Moscow. These newly unearthed objects have become part of the historical record; like documents, they are primary sources that provide clues for understanding the past. Here are some of the new findings archaeologists and historians have developed based on recently discovered Muscovite artifacts:

- Hoards of silver jewelry buried beneath the ground suggest an attempt to save valuables before the Mongol invasion of the city in 1238.
- Remains of shoes tell archaeologists that men and women in sixteenth-century Moscow were taller than we thought, averaging some five feet six inches in height, and remaining about the same until the eighteenth century.
- Ash and residue reveal the effects of a fire that burned the city to the ground in 1493 and a wooden house dating from before 1300.
- Monasteries previously unknown existed in the area around the large estates of Muscovite service nobility from the thirteenth century on.
- The kremlin (fortification) at the city center was originally built in the twelfth century with oak walls, replaced by stone forty years later.

Illustration 9.4 **Woman's Bronze Burial Decoration, 5th to 8th Century, Moscow Region**

Artifacts of old Moscow: A woman's bronze burial decoration from the Moscow region, 5th to 8th century. Does it look Russian? *(http://www.dlc.fi/~kokov/mesher/object7.jpg)*

- Archaeologists unearthed the first birchbark document ever found in Moscow. (Such documents were common around Novgorod, where the soil was waterlogged, not dry and oxidized, thus preserving the documents.)

Earlier excavations of the Kazan cathedral on Red Square, constructed in 1636, unearthed original chapels, steps, and bell tower foundations. These discoveries enabled modern builders to reconstruct the cathedral faithfully in 1993. For more on these findings, see L.A. Beliaev and A.G. Veksler, "The Archaeology of Medieval Russia: Recent Explorations (1980–1990s)," *Rossiiskaia arkheologiia* 3 (1996): 106–33.

Task: Look carefully at the bracelet illustrated here, one of the many artifacts found in Moscow. Dating from the fifth to eighth century, it is a burial bracelet worn by a woman. What can you conclude about ancient Moscow from this example? What evidence is there that this is Russian? What does the existence of a burial bracelet suggest about the people who lived there? How do artifacts resemble, and differ from, other documents and primary sources?

9.5 Images

How can images help us understand the past? When is an image a primary source? When is it secondary? We all know that photographs, sketches, graphics, paintings, and films can help us "be there" in the past. They can provide evidence of past history in ways that words on the printed page simply cannot describe. They can also help us interpret the past in new ways by letting us see things visually rather than in our imagination based on our reading.

But images—like words and maps and other items—can be deceptive. The image maker is highly selective in what he or she chooses to portray. And images can distort unless we know what lies behind them. An image may be worth a thousand words, but seeing may mean believing what is not necessarily true.

Sharpshooter's Home or Photographer's Studio?

The American Civil War (1861–1865) was one of the first conflicts to be photographed (the Crimean War in 1853–1856 was another). Developed in the 1830s, photography was a new medium that allowed people far from the battle front to visualize the bloody reality of war. Intrepid photographers like Matthew Brady and Alexander Gardner carried their heavy equipment from battle to battle to shoot pictures, which they then developed and displayed to those on the home front. Most were accurate portrayals of soldiers and war scenes—but how could viewers know for sure? Consider the case of the famous photograph taken by Alexander Gardner after the three-day Battle of Gettysburg (July 1–3, 1863), the major turning point in the war that left tens of thousand of men dead in a small Pennsylvania town and stopped the Confederate advance into the North. Gardner's photograph shows a dead Confederate soldier in the impressive cluster of boulders known by the locals as "Devil's

Illustration 9.5   **Dead Confederate Soldier in Devil's Den, Gettysburg,
July 6, 1863**

Images can be deceiving: Alexander Gardner's photograph of a dead Confederate soldier in Devil's Den, Gettysburg, July 6, 1863. Was the body moved from somewhere else? *(Library of Congress)*

Den." Devil's Den is a great hiding place and directly faces Little Round Top, another rocky hill made famous by the bloody battle that occurred there. Gardner, a Scot, and a former assistant of Matthew Brady, had established his own studio in Washington, D.C. by 1863 and hired away two of Brady's assistants, Timothy O'Sullivan and James Gibson.

Gardner and his assistants took several photographs of the battlefield on July 6, when the scene of carnage had changed very little from the days of the battle itself. They were preoccupied with dead bodies as evidence of the horrors of war. In his caption for the photograph, Gardner wrote that "the sharpshooter had evidently been wounded in the head by a fragment of a shell which had exploded over him, and had laid down upon his blanket to await death." Gardner then speculated on the soldier's mental condition as he prepared for death: "Was he delirious with agony, or did death come slowly to his relief, while memories of home grew dearer as the field of carnage faded before him?" He also remembered that when he revisited the battlefield on November 19, in connection with Lincoln's Gettysburg Address and the dedication of a federal cemetery, he discovered that "the musket, rusted by many storms, still leaned against the rock, and the skeleton of the soldier still lay undisturbed within the mouldering uniform."

It is a striking and powerful image. But historians have argued that Gardner's account of the famous photograph was not quite accurate. Other photographs suggest that this particular soldier had died elsewhere on the battlefield and that his body had been dragged some forty yards into Devil's Den for a dramatic photograph opportunity (or "photo op," as it is called today). The rifle leaning against the rocks was not the Sharps rifle used by "sharpshooters" at all, but a common infantry weapon of the period. The soldier was an infantryman, not a sharpshooter at all. There are six photographs of the body, but no log whose entries might tell us in what order Gardner took them.

The idea that this photograph was staged is now so common that tour guides at Gettysburg routinely tell the story of its staging to tourists. The National Park Service display at Devil's Den does the same thing. Revisionism has now become the conventional wisdom.

In 1975, William Frassanito, in his book *Gettysburg: A Journey in Time*, showed several photographs of the same soldier taken in different locations as much as seventy-five yards apart. He suggested that there were photographic advantages to moving a body up the hill to get a more visually exciting composition among the rocks. The photographers had even placed a knapsack under the head to prop it up. The photographer was probably not Gardner, but his assistant, Timothy O'Sullivan. At the cemetery dedication in November, photographers even got Union soldiers to "play dead" as staged bodies in Devil's Den once more.

But was the photograph staged? Perhaps the revisionists are wrong. Perhaps there really *was* a dead Confederate sharpshooter among the boulders. Other historians cite the eyewitness account of Captain August P. Martin of the Union Army artillery in the *Gettysburg Compiler* of October 24, 1899. Martin was stationed on Little Round Top:

> Among the interesting incidents that occurred on Little Round Top was the summary way in which a sharpshooter was disposed of in the

rear of Devil's Den. He had concealed himself behind a stone wall between two boulders and for a long time we were annoyed by shots from that direction, one of which actually combed my hair over my left ear and passed through the shoulder of a man a little taller than myself who was standing behind me for a cover. At last we were able to locate the spot, by the use of a field glass, from whence the shots came by little puffs of smoke that preceded the whizzing of the bullets that passed by our heads. We then loaded one of our guns with a percussion shell, taking careful and accurate aim. When the shot was fired the shell struck and exploded on the face of one of the boulders. We supposed the shot had frightened him away, as we were no longer troubled with shots from that location. When the battle was ended we rode over to the Devil's Den and found behind the wall a dead Confederate soldier lying upon his back and, so far as we could see, did not have a mark upon his body, and from that fact became convinced that he was killed by the concussion of the shell when it exploded on the face of the boulder.

So perhaps the body was in Devil's Den after all. Perhaps Gardner the photographer never had to move him at all. The debate goes on. Students interested in photographs of Gettysburg should consult William A. Frassanito, *Gettysburg: A Journey in Time* (New York: Scribner's, 1975). For a broader study, see William F. Thompson, *The Image of War: The Pictorial Reporting of the American Civil War* (Baton Rouge: Louisiana State University Press, 1959). The best account of the sharpshooter debate, from 1865 to the present, is "The Lore of the Sharpshooter" in Gary E. Edelman and Timothy H. Smith, *Devil's Den: A History and a Guide* (Gettysburg, PA: Thomas Publications, 1997).

Task: New evidence can complicate, rather than simplify, a situation, making it more difficult to verify a fact or explain the larger significance of an event. In using photographs as tools for understanding the past, what questions must historians ask of them? How might the goal of taking a poignant picture affect its "accuracy" as a document? Look carefully at Gardner's photograph. What evidence can help you decide whether the body was placed in position or not? What else do you see of any historical significance? When examining photographs, what clues might suggest that the picture was staged? In what ways, if at all, does a staged photograph—such as a president performing a certain activity—diminish its accuracy?

9.6 Cliometrics: Using Statistics to Prove a Point

Numbers are powerful tools. But how and when should historians use them? When should historians count and not count? *Cliometrics* is an amusing term used to describe the use of quantitative data (numbers, census data, election results, graphs, etc.) in the study of history. Historians often must ask the question "How much?" as well as "How?" and "Why?" For a time in the 1970s, many historians became fascinated with computers and numbers as a way of asking and answering historical questions. Quantitative history is now simply one of many tools available to the historian. Political party historians and economic historians are particularly interested in "hard data" or numbers to do their work.

The Black Population of Colonial America

In Peter Kolchin's fine book *American Slavery 1619–1877*, he needed to convey something about the relative number of black slaves in the colonies before the American Revolution. Although the numbers of blacks, or slaves, may only be approximate, he decided to discuss the

Table 9.1

Estimates of Blacks as a Percentage of the Population, by Colony, 1680–1770

	1680	1700	1720	1750	1770
Delaware	5.5	5.5	13.2	5.3	5.2
Maryland	9.0	10.9	18.9	30.8	31.5
Virginia	6.9	28.9	30.3	43.9	42.0
North Carolina	3.9	3.9	14.1	25.7	35.3
South Carolina	16.7	42.8	70.4	60.9	60.5
Georgia	—	—	—	19.2	45.2
Totals					
North	2.3	3.6	5.2	4.8	4.4
South	5.7	21.1	27.7	38.0	39.7
Thirteen Colonies	4.6	11.1	14.8	20.2	21.4

Source: Computed from *Historical Statistics of the United States: Colonial Times to 1957* (Washington, D.C.: 1960). Taken from Peter Kolchin, *American Slavery, 1619–1877* (New York: Hill and Wang, 1993), 240.

Throughout most of the seventeenth century, indentured servants filled the bulk of the colonies' labor needs. Although a Dutch captain sold twenty Africans in Virginia in 1619, and small numbers of blacks trickled into the mainland colonies over the following decades, until the 1680s the non-Indian population of the British mainland colonies remained overwhelmingly white. So long as a ready supply of indentured labor continued to exist, colonists saw little reason to go to the expense and bother of importing large numbers of Africans, who, unlike English laborers, had to undergo prolonged adjustment to alien conditions—strange masters had unusual customs and spoke an unintelligible language—before becoming productive members of the work force. Equally important, because the Portugese and Dutch dominated the African slave trade until the British triumph in the Anglo–Dutch war of 1664–67, the English colonists found slaves expensive and hard to obtain.

Beginning in the 1680s, however, the mainland colonies underwent a massive shift from indentured to slave labor. Some simple statistics drove home the point. Between 1680 and 1750, the estimated proportion of blacks in the population increased from 7 percent to 44 percent in Virginia and from 17 percent to 61 percent in South Carolina [see Table 9.1]. "They import so many Negros hither," wrote one Virginia planter, William H. Byrd II, in 1736, "that I fear this Colony will some time or other be confirmed by the Name of New Guinea."

This shift, which has been documented most carefully for the Chesapeake colonies, was the product of a fundamental change in the relative supply of indentured servants and slaves, in the face of escalating colonial demand for labor. Because servants were held only temporarily and then freed, a rapidly growing colonial population required an equally rapid growth in the number of indentured immigrants for servants to remain a constant proportion of the population. Between 1650 and 1700, the population of Virginia more than tripled; if indentured servants were to continue providing the bulk of the agricultural labor force, servant immigration would have had to triple, or come close to tripling, too.

See Peter Kolchin, *American Slavery 1619–1877* (New York: Hill and Wang, 1993), 10–11 and Table 1 (here Table 9.1).

matter in the course of his text and to provide a table at the back of his book so the reader could also draw conclusions from the data available. How does the historian's narrative relate to his quantitative data?

Are narrative and data consistent? How does he use other evidence to bolster his argument?

Task: Take a look at Table 9.1. Are the numbers here consistent with Kolchin's narrative? Are the terms and definitions used in the text and table consistent as well? Is the author selecting some data and omitting others? What other or different conclusions can you draw from the table that are not mentioned in the narrative?

9.7 Genetic Evidence

Recent technology has created a new type of evidence for historians to use in exploring the past. This evidence is genetic and is based on the DNA that exists in every human being. Because genetic material is passed on from one generation to another, historians can make strong links among people today and their ancient ancestors. By examining chromosomes, scientists can help answer questions that have long intrigued historians. DNA evidence has recently added a whole new dimension to the old debate about the relationship between President Thomas Jefferson and his slave, Sally Hemings (see next example). Similar evidence has shown conclusively that the woman who died recently in the United States who had claimed to be Anastasia—the daughter of Tsar Nicholas II of Russia—was not related to the Russian royal family, which was machine-gunned to death in August 1918 after the Bolshevik Revolution. Less sensationally, but more significantly, genetics has replaced linguistics as the tool of choice in measuring the origins of, and links among, various ethnic groups and peoples.

Welsh and Basques, Relatively Speaking

Historians have long wondered how different groups in Europe are related to each other. Because ancient records are scarce, historians have relied on linguistic evidence—that is, if the language of two geographically distinct groups share similar elements—grammar, structure, sounds—the groups are likely related. Conversely, if they do *not* share such elements, chances are they are *not* related. The Basques of northern Spain and the Welsh of Wales are two distinct groups with their own separate languages. Because these languages have little in common, historians long believed there were few links between the two groups. The Basques had been assumed, on the basis of this linguistic evidence, to be an offshoot of European aborigines from several thousand years ago. The Welsh presumably were related to the Celts, an ancient people that spread across Europe from Spain to Ireland to Romania.

But genetic evidence tells a different story. In the 1990s, scientists collected saliva samples from children in Wales, England, Italy, Germany, and Spain. After examining the DNA in these samples, geneticists discovered something astonishing. A Y chromosome very rare in England, Italy, and Germany was common in Wales, suggesting separate origins. More interesting, the Welsh Y chromosome matched Basque genes in northern Spain. Thus, the Welsh and Basques have a close biological link. DNA evidence has established a clear line of descent from common ancestors in these two separate peoples. Linguistic evidence suggested separation. Genetic evidence proves a connection.

Independently, geneticists at University College, London, were studying the population of the Orkney Islands off Scotland, where neither Anglo-Saxons nor Romans ever settled. Celtic-speaking Picts who had lived there undisturbed until the arrival of the Vikings around 800 spoke the Norse language until the eighteenth century. Genetic evidence (Y chromosomes of Orkney men) suggested an Orkney link with the Norwegians, hardly surprising.

But other genetic markers resembled those found in Welsh and Irish men, suggesting a common origin. Where? Again, geneticists compared their evidence with DNA from the Basques and, to their surprise, found the same genetic signature. Yet their study of mitochondrial DNA among women links them with northern Europe, not the Basques. Presumably females from the continent were captured, purchased, or traded and ultimately swamped the earlier genetic influences on the maternal side. So genetic evidence is an important tool and is revising history as we watch. (For more on these recent genetic discoveries, see *National Geographic*, June 2001; *New York Times*, April 10, 2001.)

Jefferson and Sally Hemings—What's My Line?

In 1776, Thomas Jefferson (1743–1826) drafted the Declaration of Independence. He later served as minister to France and secretary of state. As one of the leaders of the emerging Democratic-Republican

Party in the 1790s, he served as vice president under John Adams from 1797 to 1801 and as president of the United States from 1801 to 1809. He has long been recognized as one of the towering figures of the Revolutionary generation.

In 1772, Jefferson married Martha Wayles and took her to live at Monticello, his mountaintop home in Virginia. They had six children, only two of whom survived into adulthood, and Martha herself died in 1782. Jefferson never remarried. Like all wealthy southern plantation owners, Jefferson owned many slaves. One of them was Sally Hemings (1773–1835), about whom little is known. She left no letters or records, no images of herself. There are four known descriptions of what she looked like; she was probably light-skinned. Jefferson never mentioned her in his records. She was nursemaid and companion to Jefferson's daughter Maria, lady's maid to daughters Martha and Maria, and chambermaid and seamstress in the household. She accompanied Jefferson for more than two years in Paris and lived most of her life at Monticello. She had several children who were light-skinned:

Harriet, born 1795, died in infancy
Beverly, born 1798
Unnamed daughter, born 1799, died in infancy
Harriet, born 1801
Madison, born 1805
Eston, born 1808

Jefferson freed her surviving children—Beverly and Harriet in 1822, Madison and Eston in 1826—by his wills. He never freed Sally.

Rumors that Jefferson and Hemings had a long-standing sexual relationship abounded during their lifetimes. James T. Callender, a disappointed office seeker who wanted Jefferson to appoint him postmaster in Richmond, Virginia, printed the rumors in the *Richmond Recorder*, a Federalist newspaper, in September 1802. Jefferson "keeps and for many years has kept, as his concubine, one of his slaves," Callender charged. "Her name is Sally. The name of her eldest son is Tom. His features are said to bear a striking though sable resemblence to those of the president himself." Hemings and Jefferson "had several children," Callender wrote. "There is not an individual in the neighborhood of Charlottesville who does not believe the story."

Jefferson was a Republican. His Federalist opponents immediately pounced on the rumors and published them frequently in newspapers throughout the country. Enemies mocked him in print and in verse. The following lines, to the tune of "Yankee Doodle," appeared in the *Boston Gazette* and *Philadelphia Port Folio*:

> Of all the damsels on the green,
> On mountain or in valley,
> A lass so luscious ne'er was seen,
> As Monticellian Sally . . .
> When press'd by loads of state affairs
> I seek to sport and dally
> The sweetest solace of my cares
> Is in the lap of Sally.

Jefferson's supporters denounced the rumors and the president himself refused to respond to them. His daughter Martha denied the rumors as well, as did her children. Despite these denials, the rumors persisted until Jefferson's death in 1826. The rumors resurfaced in 1873 when sixty-eight-year-old Madison Hemings, Sally's child, said in an interview that his mother had told him that Jefferson was his father (and the father of his siblings Beverly, Harriet, and Eston). Another former slave at Monticello, Israel Jefferson, agreed.

And there the matter rested for many years. In the twentieth century, two prominent historians, Dumas Malone and Merrill Peterson, published massive biographies of Jefferson. After examining his voluminous private papers, they both repudiated the rumors for lack of evidence. Malone's biography ran to six volumes. Malone doubted the Jefferson–Hemings relationship because it was out of character for Jefferson. Another biographer, Fawn Brodie, however, provided circumstantial evidence of a Jefferson–Hemings affair. She showed that Jefferson was in residence at Monticello nine months prior to the birth of each of Sally Hemings's children and that she bore no children at times that he was not living there.

In 1997, historian Joseph Ellis raised two questions about this subject: first, Hemings's last two children were born after Callender made the issue public in 1802—how could Jefferson as president have continued their relationship following such publicity? Second, neither John

Table 9.2   Genetic Chart of Jefferson and Hemings Ancestries

A	Ancestry	B	Haplotypes		
			Bi-allelic Markers	Microsatellite STRs	Minisatellite MSY1

-Peter—Pres. Thomas Jefferson

```
                —129–135————J41        0000001  15.12.4.11.3.9.11.10.15.13.7   (3)5.(1)14.(3)32(4)16
Thomas—                  -16–112–120————
Jefferson                —130–136————J42    0000001  15.12.4.11.3.9.11.10.15.13.7   (3)5.(1)14.(3)32(4)16

          -Field————            -J13–J21–J31–J37–J43————J47   0000001  15.12.4.11.3.9.11.10.15.13.7
(3)5.(1)14.(3)32(4)16

               -J6————
                              -J46–J49  0000001  15.12.4.11.3.9.11.10.15.13.7   (3)5.(1)14.(3)32.(4)16
                  -J14–J23–J33–J39————
                              -J46–J50  0000001  15.12.4.11.3.9.11.10.16.13.7   (3)5.(1)14.(3)32.(4)16
```

Sally   Easton-H10–H15–H17————————————H210000001   15.12.4.11.3.9.11.10.15.13.7
(3)5.(1)14.(3)32.(4)16
Hemings

```
        -Thomas-C6–C11–C19–C23————————C27  0000011  14.12..5.12.3.10.11.1013.13.7
(1)17.(3)36.(4)21
John————Dabney-C8–C13–C21–C26————————C29           0000011  14.12.5.11.3.10.11.10.13.13.7
(1)17.(3)37.(4)21
Carr
        -Overton-C7–C12–C20–C24–C28–C30————————C31      0000011  14.12.5.12.3.10.11.10.13.13.7
(1)17.(3)36.(4)21

                        -W40–W55   0000011  14.12.5.11.3.10.11.13.13.13.7   (1)16.(3)27.(4)21
               -W8–W27————
                        -W41–W56   0000011  14.12.5.11.3.10.11.13.13.13.7   (1)16.(3)27.(4)21

            —Lewis—
                        -W57–W69   0000011  14.12.5.11.3.10.11.13.13.13.7   (1)16.(3)27.(4)21
Thomas                -W9–W28——W42–
Woodson————————
-W58–W80  1110001  17.12.6.11.3.11.8.10.11.14.6     (0?)1.(3e)3.(1a)11.
(3a) 30.(4a)14.(4)2

—James————W12—W30—W46————W61     0000011   14.12.5.11.3.10.11.13.13.13.7   (1)16.(3)28.(4)20
```

Note: **[For genetics students only!]** Chart shows the male-line ancestry and haplotypes of participants. A = ancestry numbers correspond to reference numbers and names in more detailed genealogical data for each family. B = haplotypes. Entries in bold highlight deviations from the usual patterns for the group of descendants. **Bi-allelic markers:** order of loci: YAP-SRYm*299 sY81–1.1.Y22g-Tat-92R7–SRYm1532. 0, ancestral state; 1, derived state. **Microsatellite short tandem repeats** (STRs). Order of loci: 19–388–389A-389B-389C-389D-390–391–392–393–dxys156y. The number of repeats at each locus is shown. **Mitnisatellite MSY1**. Each number in brackets represents the sequence type of the repeat unit; the number after it is the number of units with this sequence type. For example, J41 has 5 units of sequence type 3, 14 units of sequence type 1, 32 units of sequence type 3, and 16 units of sequence type 4.

Source: Nature, Vol. 397, November 5, 1998, 27.

Adams nor Alexander Hamilton, Jefferson's political rivals, believed the gossip—would they not have used any real evidence politically if they had? Having read all the available evidence and biographies, Ellis considered the case not proven one way or the other.

In 1998, Dr. Eugene Foster and a group of geneticists conducted a DNA study on Jefferson and Hemings descendants. Thomas Jefferson himself had no sons who sired children. But his uncle, Field Jefferson, did. The study took Y-chromosomal DNA samples from five male-line descendants of Field Jefferson, from two male descendants of Eston Hemings, and from other relatives. The study showed that there was indeed a genetic link between Jefferson and Hemings descendants. Human Y chromosomes are carried from father to son, so that all paternally related males have the identical Y chromosome. Foster's study concluded that a male with the Jefferson Y chromosome was the father of Eston Hemings, born in 1808, Sally's seventh and last child. The male-line descendants of Thomas Woodson, Sally's oldest son, did not match the DNA from the Jefferson line. Eston's DNA did. But there were twenty-five adult male Jeffersons living in Virginia within twenty miles of Monticello at the time—which one was the father? No one can know for sure, but the authors of the study concluded that Thomas Jefferson was most probably Eston Hemings's father. In January 2000, the Thomas Jefferson Foundation concurred, based on its own staff research. The foundation even suggested a high probability that Jefferson fathered six of Sally's children.

Other historians argue that Jefferson and Sally Hemings did not have any personal relationship at all. Some believe that the most likely father of Hemings's children was Jefferson's younger brother Randolph (1755–1815). So DNA as a tool may have narrowed the possibilities, but does not yet provide a definitive answer.

Whether Thomas Jefferson fathered children by Sally Hemings or not matters a great deal to their descendants, who belong to various family organizations. It also complicates our picture of Jefferson, the author of the Declaration of Independence who wrote that "all men are created equal," the plantation owner who owned slaves and believed blacks were inferior to whites, and the likely intimate companion of an African-American woman for close to forty years. The genetic evidence adds another layer of texture to the explosive and long-running issues of race relations, slavery, and interracial marriage in American history.

If you want to take the plunge into the murky waters of the Hemings–Jefferson controversy, see Joseph Ellis, *American Sphinx: The Character of Thomas Jefferson* (New York: Alfred A. Knopf, 1997), 216–19 and 303–7. Then look at Anne Gordon-Reed, *Thomas Jefferson and Sally Hemings: An American Controversy* (Charlottesville: University of Virginia Press, 1997). A more recent account is Peter S. Onuf and Jan E. Lewis, eds., *Sally Hemings and Thomas Jefferson: History, Memory, and Civic Culture* (Charlottesville: University of Virginia Press, 1999). You may also wish to look at the DNA study in the November 5, 1998 issue of *Nature.* The biographies by Malone and Peterson also offer valuable perspectives, as does Fawn Brodie's *Thomas Jefferson: An Intimate History* (New York: W.W. Norton, 1974).

Task: Write down some possible conclusions if it were proven true that Thomas Jefferson fathered children by his slave, Sally Hemings. What other examples of the use of genetic evidence for historical purposes can you find? Does genetic evidence seem reliable? What are its limits? What other kinds of evidence might be used to test its validity? What other historical controversies might genetic evidence help resolve?

10

Credit and Acknowledgment

Historians depend on their primary sources and the secondary work of other historians in order to do their work. They do not work in isolation. They must learn to credit and acknowledge the work of others so that another historian can repeat and validate (or invalidate) their work by examining the original sources that they used. The tools of acknowledgment include footnotes, bibliography, and quotation marks around the words of another person. The work of a good historian should be transparent to, and repeatable by, any other historian. Crediting and acknowledging sources is a professional and ethical responsibility for all historians. If they use or quote sources without acknowledgment, they may be accused of engaging in plagiarism or fraud.

10.1 Footnotes

Why do historians insist on diverting the reader's attention with those nagging footnotes at the bottom of the page? Why have endnotes at the back of the book? Footnotes and endnotes are a powerful tool of the historian, although students and readers often find them annoying. Footnotes or endnotes (or parenthetical citations within the text) are essential for two reasons: (1) the footnote acknowledges the source, or sources, from which the historian got information, evidence, or a quotation, enabling the reader to go to the original source to verify its accuracy or applicability; (2) the footnote permits the historian to carry on a second level of discourse with the reader that would otherwise break up the text. Footnotes do not close off, but open up, discussion and further research. They tell the reader where the historian has been and where the reader might go for further information or interpretation.

The following example shows how a historian uses an extended footnote both to acknowledge her sources and to converse with the reader about the work of two prominent historians. The author is Suzanne Desan. Her article on "Crowds, Community, and Ritual in the Work of E.P. Thompson and Natalie Davis" appeared in Lynn Hunt, ed., *The New Cultural History* (Berkeley: University of California Press, 1989), 47–71.

"By staking out new issues and methods of inquiry, E.P. Thompson and Natalie Davis have had a tremendous impact on European history, and both well deserve their outstanding reputations. No one can now work on the Reformation without reading Davis or study the Industrial Revolution without perusing Thompson. Davis's work has widened the focus of Reformation studies beyond the theological issues toward the social history of the Reformation and the examination of popular religion. Although her writing fits within the context of the Annales school, with its turn towards grassroots history and the *histoire des mentalités,* her work also complements the French approach by making greater use of symbolic anthropology and by emphasizing the crucial determining role of cultural rather than climatological, geographic, or socioeconomic factors."[1]

Task: Look at the footnote. Which parts acknowledge sources? Which parts engage the reader in a conversation? Which make specific suggestions? What might the eager reader do in response to the footnote?

---

1. In recent years, numerous *Annalistes* have shifted their point of emphasis and analysis away from long-term socioeconomic factors and toward cultural elements. On some level, the turn toward *mentalités* has even undermined the original Annales position that the critical factors were social and economic rather than cultural. See Lynn Hunt, "French History in the Last Twenty Years: The Rise and Fall of the *Annales* Paradigm," *Journal of Contemporary History* 21 (1986): 209–24, esp. p. 217. On the history of the Annales school, see Traian Stoianovich, *French Historical Method: The Annales Paradigm* (Ithaca, NY: Cornell University Press, 1976).

10.2 Bibliography

How can a bibliography be a useful tool for doing history? A bibliography is a written list of books, journal articles, or unpublished archival materials employed in the course of researching and writing a historical monograph, essay, or paper. Bibliographies normally list each entry alphabetically by the author's last name (Appleby, Joyce, under A, for example). You should keep a working bibliography on note cards as you do your research. The entry for each source used should be complete. You can then use a shorthand reference to each source at the bottom of any note card with information or text drawn from that source (Appleby, 254, for example). A bibliography is a kind of blueprint for doing history, a schematic drawing of where you or other historians have been or where you or they intend to go.

The following conventions will help you keep a working bibliography; but use your instructor's style manual for precise format.

Styling Your Bibliography

Books

Give full last name, first name, and middle name or initial of the author as it appears on the title page. Provide full book title, including subtitle, if any (in italics if you are typing). Indicate edition, if not the first. Show city of publication, publishing company, and year of publication.

Periodical Articles

Give full last name, first name, and middle name or initial of the author. Give full article title and subtitle, if any, inside quotation marks, full title of periodical (magazine, journal, newspaper, etc.) in italics, volume and issue number of periodical, month/day/year of publication in parentheses, and page numbers of the article.

Unpublished Materials

Provide full name of the archive or manuscript collection, city and state location, box number, file number, and pages if indicated.

Web Sites

Indicate author, editor, or translator, title and subject, and Internet address, e.g. http://www.xxxxxxxxxx.xxx. Also note date visited (in parentheses).

Types of Bibliographies

A bibliography may be selected, complete, or annotated. A selected bibliography lists only the most frequently consulted or significant works used in your research and is the shortest form of bibliography. A complete bibliography lists all works used in your research, even if not actually cited by you in your text. An annotated bibliography appends a phrase or sentence to each entry indicating its nature and value to you in your research. The most common form of annotated bibliography is a bibliographical essay that discusses entries in a narrative or analytical context.

A Selective, Annotated Bibliography

The following brief selection from "Note on Bibliographical Literature" comes from Benjamin Quarles, *Black Abolitionists* (New York: Oxford University Press, 1969), 251–52. Notice that it is selective, annotated, and almost historiographic. The author omits the publisher, using only city, state, and date to identify the publication. More complete publishing data as suggested in *The Chicago Manual of Style*, 14th edition, might make it easier for the reader to locate the book in question.

Notice how this bibliographical essay is selective in what it describes, descriptive of a field of study, critical of secondary sources, and suggestive of further reading. The essay shows what Quarles himself has read and what you might want to read yourself if you are interested in black abolitionists.

Bibliographies and bibliographical essays are very important tools in the reading and writing of history. They show at a glance which particular works a historian has consulted on a given topic and therefore how complete and up-to-date the research may be. Historians often begin consulting a specialized book in their field by looking first at the bibliography. You may want to do this as well.

"All students of the abolitionist movement are indebted to Dwight L. Dumond for his comprehensive *A Bibliography of Antislavery in America.* Dumond's entries are not annotated, but many of them, notably the pamphlets, bear lengthy, descriptive titles. A few items have escaped Dumond's careful attention, particularly if the conventions held by Negroes be considered of abolitionist kidney [temperament or background]. A model for the other states, the excellent *New Jersey and the Negro: A Bibliography, 1715–1966* (New Jersey Library Association, Trenton, 1967), includes a number of citations dealing with the slavery controversy, many of them relating to matters by no means confined to New Jersey. Louis Filler's thoroughly researched *The Crusade against Slavery* (New York, 1960) has a highly useful annotated bibliography designed for both the scholar and the general reader. In the fine essay on sources in his *North of Slavery: The Free Negro in the United States, 1790–1860,* Leon L. Litwack devotes one heading to white abolitionists and another to black abolitionists, in the latter emphasizing the significant role of the antebellum Negro conventions. Two works which do not list a separate bibliography but whose footnote entries are richly suggestive are Larry Gara, *The Liberty Line: The Legend of the Underground Railroad* (Lexington, Kentucky, 1961) and Charles H. Wesley, *Neglected History: Essays in Negro History by a College President* (Wilberforce, Ohio, 1965), chapters 3, 4, 5 . . ."

Task: Reread the selection from Quarles. How many different types of sources does he list? What issues does he raise about the topic of black abolitionists?

10.3 Acknowledging Sources and Avoiding Plagiarism

In all your historical work, what tools will you need to acknowledge your sources and the work of others while producing work that is truly your own? How can you avoid the sin of plagiarism? And what is plagiarism?

Plagiarism means stealing and representing another's words or ideas as one's own. These words or ideas may be few or many—a phrase, a paragraph, or several pages—but the principle is the same. Plagiarism, intentional or unintentional, is theft; it may be considered a form of lying (about one's sources) and cheating (failing to observe the ethical rules of scholarship). You need to learn to acknowledge and cite all sources properly, using quotation marks around (or indenting as a block quote) words not your own. Use footnotes, endnotes, or parenthetical citations to acknowledge the words or ideas of another. Do not plagiarize.

Consider the following paragraph from Donald Kagan, Steven Ozment, and Frank M. Turner, *The Western Heritage, Brief Edition* (Upper Saddle River, NJ: Prentice Hall, 1999), 99.

> "In 36 B.C.E. Antony attacked Parthia, and the result was disastrous. His soldiers' faith in him was further undercut when Octavian mounted a propaganda campaign that convinced them that Antony had fallen under the spell of Egypt's queen, Cleopatra. By 32 B.C.E. all pretense of cooperation came to an end. Lepidus had already been shoved aside, and at Actium in western Greece in 31 B.C.E. Octavian defeated Antony."

In this example, if you use the entire paragraph in your own paper *without* indenting or quotation marks (" ") around the paragraph (and without reference to Kagan, Ozment, and Turner 1999, 99), then you are plagiarizing from the book. If you use the entire paragraph *with* quotation marks around it and proper citation, you are not plagiarizing but neither are you writing anything in your own words. Even though you have not plagiarized and have indicated your sources, a paper with nothing but quoted paragraphs from other people is not yours either.

But these are extremes. Plagiarism is usually partial, a few words here and there, or a few sentences, or a few paragraphs. Following are two versions based on the passage from Kagan, Ozment, and Turner. Which version is plagiarized and which is paraphrased? Or are both plagiarized or both paraphrased? What is your evidence for your decision?

Version 1. The Battle of Actium (31 B.C.E.) was a major turning point in the history of Rome. We know that Antony suffered a major defeat when he took his armies into Parthia around 36 B.C.E. His great rival Octavian then undermined Antony's authority by spreading the rumor among his troops that Antony was in love with Cleopatra. Antony and Octavian completely ceased to have any kind of alliance shortly before they engaged each other at Actium. Even before Antony had lost the war to Octavian, Lepidus had been "shoved aside," according to one modern account, and Octavian had triumphed. (See Kagan 1999, 99)

Version 2. Antony attacked Parthia around 36 B.C.E. The result was disastrous. Octavian mounted a big propaganda campaign that undermined Antony's soldiers' faith in him and showed them that Antony was spellbound by Cleopatra, the queen of Egypt. By around 32 B.C.E., cooperation between Antony and Octavian was at an end. They had shoved aside Lepidus and Octavian beat Antony at Actium in 31 B.C.E.

If you still do not get the idea, there are plenty of learned scholars to help you. Begin by checking out (and reading) the Bates College Web site on plagiarism, http://www.bates.edu/pubs/plagiarism. Then try the essay by Van E. Hillier, "Acknowledging Sources and Avoiding Plagiarism," which you can find on the Duke University Web site, http://uwp.duke.edu/sources.html. There is a particularly good discussion in "Recognizing Plagiarism and Acknowledging Sources," in *The New St. Martin's Handbook* by Andrea Lunsford and Robert Connors (Boston: Bedford/St. Martin's, 1999), 494–97. Another good discussion is "Managing Information; Avoiding Plagiarism," in *The Bedford Handbook*, 5th ed., by Diana Hacker (Boston: Bedford Books, 1998), section 48, 554–62.

I hope that this brief example will help you understand how to acknowledge your sources and avoid plagiarism. In your own work, begin with your note taking. Quotation marks are your best tools. Put quotation marks around the words of others from the very beginning as you are taking notes. Then you will not think the words were your own when you review those notes. Work on developing your own arguments in your own words so you do not need to depend on the words and ideas of others. Trying to research and write a paper that is simply a compilation of the work of others is a dangerous step in the direction of plagiarism. Before you write a paper, think it through and outline it in your own words. Please do not hesitate to speak with your instructor at any time about acknowledging sources correctly and avoiding plagiarism.

Over the years I have encountered plagiarism many times among students, faculty, journalists, and politicians. Most plagiarists plead ignorance or lack of intent. But plagiarism is a serious matter in the eyes of most historians and faculty generally. You want to avoid plagiarism at all costs. The goal is to produce work that is original and truly your own, work in which you can take great pride. Your instructors and other historians stand ready to help you achieve that goal.

Task: Try to paraphrase or summarize the Kagan paragraph quoted above in a way that: (1) plagiarizes by using some of the words, phrases, or even sentences of the paragraph while following closely its structure, and without quotation marks or source acknowledgement; and (2) does not plagiarize by reorganizing, rethinking, or properly citing words, phrases, and sentences in the paragraph with reference to Kagan 1999, 99. Try both approaches and see if you can succeed in both failing and succeeding to plagiarize.

10.4 Professional Plagiarism: How Not to Do History

Could a professional historian ever plagiarize the work of other people? Astonishingly enough, even professional historians do on occasion plagiarize the work of others. In the case of two prominent writers and historians, Stephen Ambrose and Doris Kearns Goodwin, they claim innocence because others took notes for them or otherwise assisted in their work. Both have produced popular, well-written histories at a prodigious rate. Both let research assistants do much of their work. The result is sloppy research and even plagiarism. But the result is also very profitable.

The idea that one could become rich and famous by pirating the work of others is hardly new. Back in 1976, Alex Haley, the author of *Roots*, a genealogical autobiography of his African background that became a famous television series and won him the Pulitzer Prize in 1977, committed plagiarism. Haley borrowed more than eighty passages from a 1967 novel titled *The African* by Hal Courlander without attribution. Haley used these passages to concoct the fictional story of his own African ancestors whom, in fact, he did not know. Courlander settled out of court with Haley in December 1978.

Stephen Ambrose is the prolific prize-winning author of many histories and biographies, including *The Wild Blue Yonder* (New York:

Simon and Schuster, 2001), which tells the story of the United State Air Force during World War II in graphic detail. After his phenomenally popular earlier book *D Day: June 6, 1944* (New York: Simon and Schuster, 1994), carefully timed for the event's fiftieth anniversary, Ambrose formed a corporation (Ambrose and Ambrose) with his five grown sons in order to produce even more history at a faster rate. They took on jobs as his research assistants, visiting libraries, reading books, taking notes, and interviewing participants in the events described.

Sharp-eyed critics soon noticed that *Wild Blue* borrowed words and phrases from Thomas Childers, *The Wings of Morning*, and from two other books on air force history, Wesley Frank Craven and James L. Cate, *The Army Air Forces in World War II* (Chicago: University of Chicago Press, 1949) and Michael S. Sherry, *The Rise of American Air Power* (New Haven: Yale University Press, 1975). Ambrose often did not put quotation marks around the words of these other authors. He used phrases and even entire sentences verbatim without proper attribution. And he borrowed heavily from the language and logical structure as well.

For example, Childers wrote: "No amount of practice could have prepared them for what they encountered. B-24's, glittering like mica, were popping up out of the clouds all over the sky."

Ambrose wrote: "No amount of practice could have prepared the [pilot and the crew] for what they encountered [—] B-24's, glittering like mica, were popping up out of the clouds [over here, over there, everywhere.]"

When confronted with accusations, Ambrose denied that he had plagiarized. He claimed that there was "no effort to deceive." "I tell stories," he argued; "I don't discuss my documents." "I wish I had put the quotation marks in, but I didn't," he added. "I am not out there stealing other people's writings. If I am writing up a passage and it is a story I want to tell and this story fits and a part of it is from other people's writing, I just type it up that way and put it in a footnote. I just want to know where the hell it came from." Huh? Ambrose still did not get the message that borrowing the exact words of other writers is unacceptable without proper quotation and attribution.

Sherry was most generous and understanding. In an interview, he said merely that Ambrose was engaged in "sloppiness, or plagiarism, or some combination of the two." For Ambrose, the exciting and dramatic story came first. The careful and critical use of sources with correct attribution was a time-consuming nuisance.

Doris Kearns Goodwin is a popular historian and biographer of the Kennedy and Johnson families and the American presidency. In her 1987 book *The Fitzgeralds and the Kennedys* (New York: Simon and Schuster), Goodwin borrowed entire passages and sentences word for word from Lynne McTaggart's biography, *Kathleen Kennedy: Her Life and Times* (New York: Dell, 1983). When McTaggart threatened to sue for copyright infringement, Goodwin settled out of court. Simon and Schuster in 1987 paid off McTaggart and destroyed all copies of its inventory of Goodwin's book (The publishing company plans to correct errors and republish the book, of course, thereby making more money.)

McTaggart wrote recently that she was "shocked to read passage after passage of my own book embedded in hers." "In my case," she said, "whether Ms. Goodwin had used footnotes or even quotation marks around the passages taken from my book would not have mattered. (Some passages were credited to me in footnotes.) It was the sheer volume of appropriation—thousands of my exact or nearly exact words—that supported my copyright infringement claim." (Letter to *New York Times*, March 16, 2002, A27.)

But Goodwin also failed to place quotation marks around sentences taken from Hank Searls, *The Lost Prince: Young Joe, the Forgotten Kennedy* (New York: New American Library, 1969) and his *Rose Kennedy: Times to Remember* (New York: Doubleday, 1974). She explained that the problem was in her handwritten notes from years earlier, which she failed to check. "I should have had the books in front of me," she added, with respect to McTaggart's book. "I failed to provide quotation marks for phrases that I had taken verbatim having assumed that these phrases, drawn from my notes, were my words, not hers. . . . I wrote everything in longhand in those days, including the notes I took on secondary sources. . . . Drawing on my notes, I did not realize that in some cases they constituted a close paraphrase of the original work." Again, Goodwin seems to miss the point. Unintentional theft is still theft.

These cases of plagiarism all vary in intent and method. Alex Haley borrowed passages without attribution from a novel in order to describe an ancestor that never existed. Stephen Ambrose (or his research assistants) borrowed passages without attribution from various air force histories and added his own style for flavoring. Doris Kearns Goodwin

Illustration 10.1 **Cartoon, Historian Stephen Ambrose and Philosopher George Santayana**

How could they? Professional Plagiarism: Historian Stephen Ambrose and philosopher George Santayana write on . . . in identical prose *(Kevin Siers/ Reprinted with special permission of North American Syndicate)*

used passages without attribution ostensibly because she took notes without using quotation marks in the first place. Haley, Ambrose, and Goodwin have many things in common: they write well, they employ others to do their research, they produce large amounts of prose, they make large amounts of money, and they plagiarize. They have admitted their plagiarism with varying degrees of candor. They write popular history for a mass audience, and they are very poor practitioners of the professional historian's trade.

Haley, Ambrose, and Goodwin got caught doing what any college student of history is constantly reminded to avoid: they plagiarized. As historians, they are not worthy of emulation.

If you wish to find out more about professional plagiarism, see David D. Kirkpatrick's articles on Ambrose in the *New York Times*, January 5, 13, and 25, 2002. Also Paul Gray, "Other People's Words," *Smithsonian Magazine* 32: 12 (March 2002): 102–3. On Goodwin, see *Time*, February 4, 2002, and Gray, "Words," 103. On Haley, see Philip Nobile, *The Village Voice*, February 23, 1993.

Task: Look again at the examples of Haley, Ambrose, and Goodwin.

Exactly how are they plagiarizing? How do they differ from, or resemble, each other in the way they have failed to acknowledge sources properly?

10.5 Using the Internet: Promises and Pitfalls

The Internet is one of the historian's newest tools. How can the Internet help you and other historians do your work? What are the benefits and risks of Internet research? Clearly the Internet places more information in the hands of historians than ever before. Internet sites abound for every specialized interest imaginable. You can search the bibliographies and catalogs of libraries and archives all over the world. Recent runs of journals exist on-line. Old documents are cataloged online and even available to print out on your own computer.

Here are a few helpful sites to get you started:

- *History News Network* http://chnm.gmu.edu/hun offers a massive number of links to history sites sponsored by the Center for History and New Media.
- *Reviews in American History* http://muse.jhu.edu/journals/ reviews_in_American_history provides review articles for students of American history.
- *Library of Congress American Memory* http://memory.loc.gov/ ammem/mdbquery.html gives a fantastic range of documents and images from American history and culture.
- *Institute of Historical Research, University of London, History On-Line* http://ihr.sas.ac.uk/search/welcome.html shows links to hundreds of sites worldwide of interest to historians.
- *National Union Catalogue of Manuscript Collections* http:// lcweb.loc.gov/coll/nucmc.html provides links with every major manuscript collection in the United States.
- *British Library A2A Database* http://www.a2a.pro.gov.uk/lists hundreds of archival sites in the United Kingdom.
- *Making of America (Michigan)* http://moa.umdl.umich.edu indexes and often reproduces in entirety primary sources, including journals and journal articles, focusing on nineteenth-century American social history.
- *Archiving Early America* http://www.earlyamerica.com has an enormous amount of primary source material from the eighteenth century.

- *National Archives and Records Administration Information Locator (NAIL)* http://www.nara.gov/nara/nailhi.html provides more than 600,000 descriptions of archival holdings.

Internet sites are often criticized for being uncritical, self-published, and not peer reviewed. Surely one must be careful (as with published material). But the historical material available today on the Internet is simply unprecedented. The Internet is a major tool of any working historian and history student. Most historians use the Internet as a starting point for research and bibliographical aids; however, there is no substitute for the library and the archive.

An excellent guide to the Internet for historians is Dennis A. Trinkle and Scott A. Merriman, eds., *The History Highway 3.0* (Armonk, NY: M.E. Sharpe, 2002), which runs to 672 pages and provides descriptions of thousands of Web sites. An accompanying CD-ROM includes live links to every site.

Task: Log on to an Internet site devoted to some aspect of history. Who created the site? Was the site peer reviewed? How does the site relate to books and articles found in a library? Does the site tell you any more than printed sources?

11

Narrative and Explanation

History involves both telling a story and explaining how, or why, events occurred as they did. Historians narrate and explain the past in ordinary language of their own day—language which changes over time. They normally follow a sequence of events in chronological order. But they may also start with the end, rather than the beginning, of the story to achieve dramatic effect. After all, historians already know the outcome of the story they intend to tell, unlike the actual historical participants in the events being narrated. Historians must try to explain what caused the events in their story—the reasons why events happened the way that they did—without ignoring the free choices made by historical actors at the time.

11.1 The Language of the Historian

Language is a tool for writing. What kind of language should you expect to encounter as you read history? What kind of language should you use when you write history? Historians tend to write in ordinary language that ordinary people can read and understand. This is certainly a charm of the craft of history. Most people cannot pick up an issue of a scientific or social science journal and begin to understand the esoteric, technical, often quantitative and complex language of the discipline. History is different.

Historians try to write in a language that both captures the spirit of the historical period, event, or character and that appeals to a contemporary audience. The language of the historian is normally simple, direct, and comprehensible, however complex the evidence or argument may be. Most people can read and enjoy history because it uses ordinary language. Using ordinary language well is therefore one of the historian's most important tools.

Paul Revere and the New England Village

Language changes over time. Two historians separated by more than a century may well describe the same event but in a different language. Consider the well-known "midnight ride" of Boston silversmith Paul Revere on April 18, 1775, to warn the citizens, especially armed "minute men," of the area around Boston that "redcoats"—British soldiers— were going to march on the nearby towns of Lexington and Concord to seize stores of arms and ammunition hidden by American patriots. Friends rowed Revere across the Charles River in a boat around ten o'clock at night. He then mounted a horse and rode west to Lexington, Lincoln, and Concord. Revere and his friend William Dawes were only two of dozens of riders out that night. But Paul Revere's midnight ride is part of American folklore. Inventor Thomas Edison even made a film about it as early as 1914.

Below are two different accounts of Paul Revere's ride, one written by mid-nineteenth-century historian George Bancroft, one written by late twentieth-century historian David Hackett Fischer. As you read them, consider how they differ. How are they similar? How is their language different? Similar? What does each emphasize? What facts do they present? Can you tell which was written by Bancroft and which by Fischer? How do their approaches differ? What clues reveal the era in which each account was written?

Here is the solution: Account 1 is by Bancroft, from his massive *History of the United States from the Discovery of the American Continent*, 9 vols. (Boston: Little, Brown, 1857–1866), vol. 7, 289–91. Account 2 is by Fischer from *Paul Revere's Ride* (New York: Oxford University Press, 1994, 130), an entire monograph devoted to the story. Bancroft writes a flowing narrative in plain English. According to Bancroft, two dispatch riders, Paul Revere and William Dawes, rode off around ten o'clock in the evening to sound the alarm. He then describes how British officers finally seized Revere and Dawes when they got as far as Lincoln, then took them back to Lexington and released them.

Account 1

"Revere stopped only to engage a friend to raise the concerted signals, and five minutes before the sentinels received the order to prevent it, two friends rowed him past the Somerset man of war across the Charles River. All was still, as suited the hour. The ship was winding with the young flood; the waning moon just peered above a clear horizon; while from a couple of lanterns in the tower of the North Church, the beacon streamed to the neighboring towns, as fast as light could travel. . . .

Express messengers and the call of minute-men spread widely the alarm. How children trembled as they were scared out of sleep by the cries! How wives with heaving breasts, bravely seconded their husbands; how the countrymen, forced suddenly to arm, without the guides or counselors, took instant counsel of their courage. The mighty chorus of voices rose from the scattered farmhouses, and as it were from the very ashes of the dead. Come forth, champions of liberty; now free your country; protect your sons and daughters, your wives and homesteads; rescue the houses of the God of your fathers, the franchises handed down from your ancestors. Now all is at stake; the battle is for all."

Account 2

"Two miles beyond Lexington Green, they entered the town of Lincoln, a new community that had been created only twenty years before. Paul Revere reckoned they had come 'about half way from Lexington to Concord.' Here the Great Road curved westward through open fields and pastures, interspersed with patches of swamp and woodland. Very near the boundary between Lincoln and Lexington, the road ran past a little cluster of farmsteads, three or four of them, a few hundred feet apart. Each house was set only a few feet from the north edge of the highway, facing south toward the warmth of the sun, according to the Yankee custom. All were occupied by families called Nelson. This pattern of settlement was typical of old New England. It was the custom for sons to settle close to their father's land, while the daughters moved away. As a consequence, many town centers in Massachusetts were surrounded by small hamlets of households with the same surname."

Illustration 11.1 **The Midnight Ride of Paul Revere**

"Great patriot" or "dead white male on a horse"? *The Midnight Ride of Paul Revere* by William Robinson Leigh suggests visually the changing language of historians over time. *(Library of Congress)*

Bancroft's language is dramatic, charged with emotion and patriotism, part of the long narrative of American history, full of details about the time and the weather, imagining the response of women and children to the alarm. The citizens of Boston are "champions of liberty." Their resistance to British domination is God-given and ancestral. This is nationalist, narrative history at its nineteenth-century best. Fischer writes from a different, more modern perspective, reminding readers that "the saga of the midnight ride is one of many shared memories that make Americans one people, diverse as we may be." He notes that professional historians have largely ignored the ride as too patriotic, too "politically incorrect," the narrative about a "dead white male on horseback." Many contemporary historians have abandoned the study of individuals and events for social history, culture, and material artifacts. Fischer seeks to retell the story of Paul Revere's ride using the language of social history, as well as telling the story of one individual.

Notice how Fischer switches from the story of Paul Revere sounding the alarm to the story of New England town settlement and society. All of a sudden we find ourselves not simply in Lincoln, but in a typical New England town, learning about land settlement, family life, and farm building patterns. We have moved from Bancroft's patriotic story of one "great man" to a glimpse into New England society and culture.

In the end, Fischer gives us the most complete and authoritative study of Paul Revere's ride ever written. We learn that Revere and Dawes were only two of dozens of alarm riders out that night in a well-organized effort to alert the countryside. We learn that people did not shout "The British are coming," because they were virtually all British citizens at the time; rather, they shouted "The redcoats are out." And we learn about artifacts—Revere's saddlebags and eyeglasses, firearms and field guns, houses and churches—about how society was organized, and about the mythical interpretations of Revere's ride as exemplified in Henry Wadsworth Longfellow's famous poem, "The Midnight Ride of Paul Revere" (1863) and the painting by William Robinson Leigh. Drawing on the language and research of his fellow historians, Fischer gives us quite a new and equally dramatic story of Paul Revere's ride with less emphasis on patriotism and more on historical contingency. What if Revere and Dawes had never gotten across the Charles River that night? Would American history have been different?

Both Bancroft and Fischer describe Revere's ride in clear, flowing prose using the ordinary language of their day. But individual liberty and national pride in the first account have given way to social history and microhistorical detail in the second account. Ordinary language and historical technique have both changed dramatically in the past century and a half.

The language of the historian changes over time, along with the language of the culture in which the historian resides. Historians today would not use the phrase "great men" so beloved of nineteenth-century historians. They try to write in a language that is gender-neutral, race-neutral, and inoffensive. They emphasize social structure more than individual human agency. Historical language tends to follow social and cultural norms. The example of Paul Revere's famous ride, and his role as part of a committee of dispatch riders to small New England towns that famous night, alert us to the changing language and thinking of historians over time. Historians use ordinary language, but ordinary language changes.

Task: What are the merits of the two different accounts of the same event presented by Bancroft and Fischer? Which account seems more effective to you? Why? Look closely at William Robinson Leigh's painting of Paul Revere's ride. Does the painting reflect the language of Bancroft, or Fischer, or both, or neither? Why? Do you see a lone rider or a New England town at first glance?

11.2 Chronology

A chronology lists events over time in order. What kind of tool is a chronology? How can a chronology help you organize your material when you write a paper? Doing a chronology can be a very helpful intermediate step in researching and writing your history paper, especially in producing a narrative. Keep a chronology as you take notes on cards. Keep notes in chronological order (you may wish to reorder them as your ideas develop). After doing some of your research, do a chronology to help you order events and see possible patterns. A good chronology can be a great help when you come to do the first draft of your paper. A chronology also helps as a reference point during both the research and writing process.

The Life of Margaret Fuller

As an example, consider a brief chronology of the life of Margaret Fuller (1810–1850), a pioneer literary critic, writer, and journalist, colleague of Ralph Waldo Emerson, and author of *Woman in the Nineteenth Century*. The chronology is taken from Mary Kelley, ed., *The Portable Margaret Fuller* (New York: Penguin, 1994).

Illustration 11.2 **Margaret Fuller, 1846**

The only known photograph taken of Margaret Fuller, 1846. *(The Granger Collection, New York)*

Notice how the historian limits her entries to the most significant events (I have reduced the entries even further). We know a great deal about Margaret Fuller's life. These are only a few of her most notable activities, publications, and travels. Any chronology is highly selective and excludes many events, including events that could give context to the life. The last entry can hardly convey the sadness and grief with which Margaret Fuller's many friends responded to her tragic and untimely death with Osoli and their infant son.

If you were to write a biography of Fuller, this chronology would constitute a helpful reference tool. Chronology reminds you what happened when and in what order. But it is only a chronology—a list of

Chronology

1810   Sarah Margaret Fuller is born in Cambridgeport, Massachusetts on May 23.

1824   Begins a year as a student at Miss Prescott's Young Ladies' Seminary in Groton, Massachusetts.

1825   Returns to Cambridge, Massachusetts.

1833   Moves to Groton, Massachusetts, with family and tutors her younger siblings Richard, Arthur, and Lloyd. Translates Goethe's *Torquato Tasso*.

1836   Begins teaching at Bronson Alcott's Temple School in Boston.

1837   Moves to Providence, Rhode Island, to teach at the Greene Street School.

1838   Resigns position at the Greene Street School.

1839   Publishes her translation of *Eckermann's Conversations with Goethe*. Continues research on a biography of Goethe. Agrees to edit newly founded Transcendentalist periodical *Dial*. Begins series of classes, or "Conversations," for adult women.

1840   Begins "Autobiographical Sketch." Edits *Dial* from July until July of 1842.

1842   Publishes "Bettine Brentano and Her Friend Gunderode" in *Dial*.

1844   Concludes final series of "Conversations." Publishes *Summer on the Lakes, during 1843*. Moves to New York City and begins literary editorship of Horace Greeley's *New-York Daily Tribune*.

1845   Publishes *Woman in the Nineteenth Century*.

1846   Resigns literary editorship and accepts position as foreign correspondent for the *New-York Daily Tribune*. Sails for Europe with Marcus and Rebecca Spring. Publishes first dispatch in *New-York Daily Tribune* on September 24. Travels in England, Scotland, and France.

1847   Leaves France for Italy in February. Arrives in Rome and meets Giovanni Angelo Ossoli in April. Travels in northern Italy and Switzerland from July to October. Begins residence in Rome in October.

1848   Angelo Ossoli is born in Rieti on September 5. Pellegrino Rossi is assassinated and Pope Pius IX flees from Rome in November.

1849   Roman Republic is proclaimed in February. Siege of Rome by the French begins in April. French invade Rome and restore Pope to power in June. Fuller, Ossoli, and their son, Angelo, move to Florence in November.

1850   Publishes her final dispatch in *New-York Daily Tribune* on February 13. Sails for the United States with Ossoli and Angelo on May 17. Dies in shipwreck off Fire Island on July 19.

highlights and milestones—not a narrative or a biography. You need to connect the dots, so to speak, and develop an argument to make chronology come alive in a significant way. This example is simplistic because it begins with the subject's birth and ends with her death. When you should begin and end a chronology is usually much more complex.

Chronology is a limited but important tool that you can use to do history. It is the skeleton on which narrative and interpretation will put flesh. You will find chronology helpful both in organizing your notes and in beginning to write.

Task: Write a brief chronology of your own life. What events should you include? What should you exclude? Why? What does the chronology reveal about your life? What does it not reveal?

11.3 Narrative

Telling a story or writing a narrative is one of the historian's most essential tools. Narrative moves beyond chronology. It selects, explains, and interprets events even while it sets them in some chronological order. How can you write a good narrative while keeping sight of your overall argument? Narratives are normally true stories of historical events in chronological sequence. They may be long or short, but they should not be isolated from the argument, thesis, or main point of your paper. Your paper should be neither entirely narrative nor analytic, but a creative combination of both approaches.

Pickett's Charge at Gettysburg

As an example, consider the problem facing James McPherson, the premier historian of the Civil War. In his prize-winning book *Battle Cry of Freedom: The Civil War Era* (New York: Oxford University Press, 1988), he covered not only the war itself, but the decades leading up to that "irrepressible conflict." When he came to the Battle of Gettysburg (July 1–3, 1863), the major turning point in the war, he had to deal in brief with a topic on which dozens, if not hundreds, of books have been written. Even covering Pickett's famous charge against the Union batteries was a challenge. He could have written hundreds

Illustration 11.3 **The Aftermath of Pickett's Charge at Gettysburg, July 4, 1863**

After Pickett's charge: How do you write a narrative when most of the participants are dead? (*Library of Congress*)

"With Pickett's fresh division as a spearhead, therefore, [Confederate general Robert E.] Lee would send three divisions preceded by an artillery barrage against that weakened center on July 3 [1863]. [Confederate general J.E.B.] Stuart would circle around the Union rear and [Union general Richard] Ewell would assail the right flank to clamp the pincers when Pickett broke through the front. With proper coordination and leadership, his invincible troops could not fail.

Across the way a midnight council of Union generals resolved to stay and fight it out. With prescience, [Union general George] Meade told the general commanding his center that 'if Lee attacks to-morrow, it will be in *your front*.' At first light, however, fighting broke out at the extreme right of the Union line, along the base of Culp's Hill. Units of the Federal 12th Corps, which had been shifted to the left the previous day, came back during the night and attacked at dawn to regain their abandoned trenches now occupied by the rebels. In a seven-hour firefight they succeeded, and thus dimmed Lee's chances for turning the Union right simultaneously with the planned piercing of the center.

While this was going on, [Confederate general James] Longstreet once more urged Lee to maneuver around Meade's left. Again Lee refused, and ordered Longstreet to attack the Union center with Pickett's division and two of Hill's—fewer than 15,000 men to advance three-quarters of a mile across open fields and assault dug-in infantry supported by ample artillery. 'General Lee,' Longstreet later reported himself to have said, 'there never was a body of fifteen thousand men who could make that attack successfully.'

In this mood, Longstreet ordered a concentration of Confederate artillery—some 150 guns—for the largest southern bombardment of the war, to soften up the enemy at the point of attack. At 1:07 P.M. Longstreet's guns shattered the uneasy silence that had followed the morning's fight on the Union right. For almost two hours an artillery duel among nearly 300 guns filled the Pennsylvania countryside with an ear-splitting roar heard as far away as Pittsburgh. Despite this sound and fury, the Union infantry lying behind stone walls and breastworks suffered little, for the rebel aim was high.

Pickett's all-Virginia division waited with nervous impatience to go in and get it over with. Thirty-eight years old, George Pickett had graduated last in the same West Point class as [former Union general] George McClellan (who graduated second). . . . With his long hair worn in ringlets and his face adorned by a drooping mustache and goatee,

Pickett looked like a cross between a Cavalier dandy and riverboat gambler. He affected the romantic style of Sir Walter Scott's heroes and was eager to win everlasting glory at Gettysburg.

Finally, about 3:00 P.M., Longstreet reluctantly ordered the attack. The Confederate bombardment seemed to have disabled the enemy's artillery; it was now or never. With parade-ground precision, Pickett's three brigades moved out joined by six more from Hill's division on their left and two others in reserve. It was a magnificent mile-wide spectacle, a picture-book view of war that participants on both sides remembered with awe until their dying moment—which for many came within the next hour. Pickett's charge represented the Confederate war effort in microcosm: matchless valor, apparent initial success, and ultimate disaster. As the gray infantry poured across the gently undulating farmland with seemingly irresistible force, northern artillery suddenly erupted in a savage cascade, sending shot and shell among the southern regiments and changing to canister as they kept coming. . . . Yankee infantry behind stone walls opened up at 200 yards while Vermont, Ohio, and New York regiments on the left and right swung out to rake both flanks of the attacking force. The southern assault collapsed under this unbearable pressure from front and flanks. Two or three hundred Virginians and Tennesseans with General Lewis A. Armistead breached the first Union line, where Armistead was mortally wounded with his hand on a Yankee cannon and his followers fell like leaves in an autumn wind. In half an hour it was all over. Of the 14,000 Confederates who had gone forward, scarcely half returned. Pickett's own division lost two-thirds of its men; his three brigadiers and all thirteen colonels were killed or wounded."

of pages; he gave himself two. Somehow he had to make the narrative significant and dramatic, infusing it with meaning, while keeping it short. The result is above. Did he succeed?

Somehow, the historian here uses narrative as a tool to convey the "sound and fury" of combat along with the visual images of terrain and men at arms, the training of soldiers, the struggle between the industrial North and the agrarian South, and the romance and reality of battle. The narrative is spare and concise, yet rich in meaning and implication. It is tense, dramatic, and detailed. Anyone who has walked the ground and seen the monuments to the so-called "high-water mark of the Confederacy" understands what McPherson has accomplished. We should all write narrative history so well.

Notice, however, that the established facts about Pickett's charge are few. We do not know the exact number of Confederate soldiers involved in the charge at all. Most soldiers at Gettysburg were not involved in the charge. Most of those involved were killed. The survivors lived to tell their stories, to memorialize the past, and to share memories at the subsequent reunions of Gettysburg veterans, North and South. Narrative can often raise more questions than it answers. What questions does this narrative of Pickett's charge suggest to you?

If you want to see how Pickett's charge—this brief but significant event—has been continually reexamined and reinvented ever since July 3, 1863, read Carol Reardon, *Pickett's Charge in History and Memory* (Chapel Hill: University of North Carolina Press, 1997). The account here is reprinted with permission of Oxford University Press from James McPherson, *Battle Cry of Freedom: The Civil War Era* (New York: Oxford University Press, 1988), 661–62.

Task: Write your own brief narrative of Pickett's charge using only the information provided by McPherson in his account of this famous event. How is your narrative distinct from McPherson's? What did you include? What did you leave out?

11.4 Argument

Argument is another important tool of the historian. How is history an argument, as well as a story? Like lawyers, historians argue a case before their peers, that is, other historians. The logic of a good argument lies beneath the surface of any good work of history. In your papers, you will want to develop an argument based upon the evidence you discover and construct to tell your story. You will need to persuade the reader that your conclusion follows from your premises, your evidence, and your argument.

An argument is an attempt to support a conclusion with reasons and evidence. An argument is not an assertion, nor is it an opinion, nor is it simply part of a dispute. Not all arguments are equal. Some are more persuasive than others. An argument begins with premises, reliable statements giving reasons. A conclusion is a final statement. Arguments may be based on (1) examples and evidence; (2) analogies (not very persuasive among historians); (3) authority (e.g., your sources). You will want to show how your argument fits into the historiography of other historians writing on your subject and how it relates to their arguments.

Watch out for fallacies when engaged in an argument. For example, do not generalize on the basis of incomplete or insufficient evidence. Do not overlook alternative explanations. Avoid confusing the correlation of two events with the causation of one event by the other. For a good introduction to the nature of argument, which also specifies various fallacies, see Anthony Weston, *A Rulebook for Arguments*, 2d ed. (Indianapolis: Hackett Publishers, 1992).

"Little Women" Who Helped Make This Great War

Arguments may appear in a paragraph, a chapter, or a book. Here is a brief example of an argument from Glenna Matthews, "'Little Women' Who Helped Make This Great War," in Gabor S. Boritt, ed., *Why the Civil War Came* (New York: Oxford University Press, 1996), 44:

> "The abolitionist women's willingness to attend notorious trials involving the status of African-Americans attempting to attain their freedom in Northern courts provided another means for shaping public opinion. [*premise*] In effect, such women risked their reputations for respectability in order to dramatize their support of oppressed people. Says the legal historian Paul Finkelman: [*authority*] 'As spectators women abolitionists unnerved proslavery jurists and lawyers. In this role they were effective because their very presence in the courtroom challenged the prevailing role of women.' But the women went further. Finkelman describes how 'the Boston Female Anti-Slavery Society initiated litigation on behalf of the cause.' For example, [*evidence*] in 1836 they were 'spark-plugs' in bringing to the courts the case of Med, a six-year-old slave girl who had come to Boston with her owner.[12] [*footnote to work cited as authority*]
>
> By means both dramatic and subtle, then, abolitionist women undertook to shape public opinion in the years preceding the war." [*conclusion*]

Please note that arguments are rarely so clear and present as in this example. Try to find some yourself as you read. Check their logic. Check your own logic too.

Task: Write down an argument about a historical event of your own choosing. Make sure that the argument contains evidence, reasons, and a conclusion. Are you persuaded?

11.5 Causation

Causes are the tools of historical explanation. How do causes help explain the past? A cause is something that produces an effect, action, or event. The force of gravity, for example, causes a ball to roll down an inclined plane. Historians use causation to explain why, or how, an event happened. Since history involves the study of change over time, causes must precede events chronologically. Historians often distinguish between necessary and sufficient causes. A necessary cause is a cause that had to happen if the caused event were ever to occur. Without that cause, the event would not have happened. A sufficient cause is a cause that led to the event only because the necessary causes were already present at the time.

For example, historians trying to explain why the Civil War occurred must first make clear which event, or trend, they are explaining: (1) the sectional division between North and South, the states that fought each other in the war; (2) the secession of southern states in 1860 and 1861; or (3) the outbreak of the war itself in April 1861. Assuming they want to explain the actual outbreak of war, historians would consider the following necessary causes (or conditions). Without these necessary causes, the war would not have occurred:

1. Slavery: the institution of slavery in the South made the cultivation of cotton and tobacco crops economically profitable. Slavery employed unpaid labor, which competed with free wage labor in the North. Abolitionists considered slavery immoral and evil. They wanted to abolish it as soon as possible. Southerners felt threatened economically and socially by northern intervention and abolition of slavery. The United States was divided into free and slave states.
2. States' rights: the doctrine that the United States was formed

as a compact among individual states, any one of which could nullify that compact if it decided that the federal government interfered too much in the state's internal affairs.

3. Sectionalism: North and South had many disagreements and divisions apart from slavery, especially about the many tariffs imposed by northern manufacturers on goods purchased in the South. In addition, the sections had distinct agricultural and industrial economies, different value systems, and different ways of life.

4. Cultural differences and perceptions: Many people in the North and the South came to believe hostile stereotypes about each other. Politicians stereotyped the sections as southern "slavocracy" or northern "black Republicans." Southern honor confronted Yankee ingenuity. In this case, what people believed was happening before the Civil War came to be as important as what did actually happen.

Given these *necessary* causes for a civil war between North and South, what constituted a *sufficient* cause for war? Many people had been predicting a civil war for decades. In 1858, New York senator William H. Seward referred to the sectional controversy as an "irrepressible conflict between opposing and enduring forces." Earlier in the century, several states had threatened to secede from the Union (for example, New England in the Hartford Convention of 1814, and South Carolina in the nullification crisis of 1832). There had been bloody slave revolts (Nat Turner in Virginia in 1831) and dramatic attempts to incite a slave rebellion (John Brown in 1859). There had been moments of crisis such as the Mexican War of 1846–1848 and the Kansas–Nebraska Act of 1854. But a series of compromises, notably the Missouri Compromise of 1820 and the Compromise of 1850, had headed off conflict, so that various possible causes of a civil war turned out to be insufficient.

But the tensions and sectional divisions always existed, especially in the 1840s and 1850s. What finally sparked the Civil War? *Sufficient* causes for the war included (1) the election of Abraham Lincoln in 1860 because he was the first candidate of a political party resolved to stop the spread of slavery to become president; (2) the secession of southern states from the Union in late 1860 and early 1861 because it dissolved the Union with the North; (3) the resupplying of, and firing upon, Fort Sumter in Charleston Harbor in April 1861, because these were viewed as acts of war by either South or North. These causes would not have been sufficient to produce civil war unless they combined with the already existing *necessary* causes listed above.

Historians who accept the conventional wisdom that the Civil War became, after a point, an "irrepressible conflict" tend to emphasize necessary causes. In their view, the war was inevitable: it could be delayed but not postponed. Other historians reject the conventional wisdom in favor of the view that a few historical actors—militant abolitionists who condemned slavery, "fire-eating" southerners who denounced abolitionists, and "bungling politicians" who failed to resolve the dispute peacefully—brought on the Civil War by their actions. In this view, the war was not at all inevitable, but could have been avoided had a few leaders acted differently and sought compromise instead of conflict.

Historians also distinguish between monocausal (slavery) and multicausal (sectionalism, the tariff, western expansion, slavery, perceptions) explanations of the Civil War. Most historians take a multicausal approach, admitting the existence of more than one possible cause of any given event.

A good examination of the topic of causation is Kenneth M. Stampp, ed., *The Causes of the Civil War* (New York: Simon and Schuster, 1959), which includes both primary and secondary sources.

Task: Write a sentence in which you attribute the Civil War to a single cause. Now write another sentence in which you attribute the war to many different causes. Which sentence seems more persuasive to you? Why? How would you go about demonstrating your point? What evidence would you look for?

11.6 The Reasons Why

Explanation is a powerful tool of the historian. Explaining why, or how, events happened the way that they did is central to the historian's craft. Explaining an event means providing evidence of the reasons why that event happened. But what constitutes a good explanation? Exactly what is being explained?

Explaining the Mann Gulch Fire of August 5, 1949

One of the best examples I know of how to explain a historical (and natural) event is contained in writer Norman Maclean's famous book titled *Young Men and Fire*. Published by the University of Chicago Press in 1992, after Maclean's death, the book tells the story of eighteen young smoke jumpers, most of whom perished trying to extinguish a forest fire in rugged Mann Gulch along the Missouri River north of Helena, Montana, in the hot, dry summer of 1949. A master craftsman who knew the area from his own youth, Maclean tells not only a tragic story in a compelling manner, but also the parallel story of how he, as a historian and writer, tried to find out what actually happened. He asks many questions and employs a number of techniques to help explain why, and how, a forest fire blew up and young men died terribly of burns and asphyxiation in a fire.

What Happened?

Maclean is a great storyteller. He describes the young smoke jumpers in loving detail, their training, their barroom brawls, their self-confident sense of immortality, their jump from a noisy, bouncing airplane into a fire from 2,000 feet, in high winds and at a temperature of ninety-seven degrees. He tells how a brush fire became spot fires, then crown fires at the tops of trees, then a "blowup" of a fast-moving inferno.

What Is the Evidence?

Maclean soon discovers that the official Forest Service report of the incident conceals as much as it reveals. He conducts interviews, he visits the archives to examine documents. He gathers data about wind and temperature from the old weather reports. He finds maps and photographs.

What Was It Like?

Maclean knew Montana from his youth. He had fought fires himself. Several decades later, he returns to the scene of the fire, where only charred ash and crosses marking deaths remain. He climbs the gulch, retraces old routes with survivors and witnesses, pores over old records and pictures. He tries to imagine what it was like to be eighteen and scared and jumping into a conflagration. He remembers his wife, dying of emphysema, gasping for oxygen.

Why Did Some Survive and Others Perish?

Maclean interviews two survivors of the fire, Walter Rumsey and Robert Sallee, to discover how they made it out alive. They were the youngest members of the crew (at eighteen), but had plenty of experience. He concludes that they had advantages of strength and speed, but also some good luck. He also examines the chain of recruiting, training, and decisions by the Forest Service that brought the men into that fire that day and led most to their untimely death.

Why Did the Fire Blow Up?

Here Maclean turns to science. He visits a fire science laboratory. He learns about many different types of fires. He reads about winds and wind currents in mountainous terrain, updrafts and downdrafts. He maps the wind currents on the day of the fire. He plots the velocity of the fire against the time of death of men found with melted watches on their bodies. He graphs annual fire statistics to see the impact of the introduction of smoke jumpers into fire fighting. He cross-checks the location of every cross on the hillside to establish who died where and when.

How Did Three Men Escape?

Interviews showed that Rumsey and Sallee had somehow found their way uphill and sideways to a ridge of rock formations along the top of the gulch. They located crevices and squeezed through to safety. A third man died of his burns after making it through. Maclean learns how the foreman, Wag Dodge, used an old Native American technique of lighting a backfire in the grass around him so that the main fire leapfrogged over him. Dodge alone survived in the gulch.

Did the Backfire Save Lives or Kill Young Men?

When the father of one of the men killed in the fire sued the Forest Service, he argued in court that Wag Dodge's backfire may have saved

Dodge, but killed his son when it became a branch of the main fire. Maclean used fire science and evidence from the melted watches to argue that the main fire, not the escape fire, finally caught up with the other men as they raced uphill pursued by a roaring fire fanned by twenty-mile-an-hour dry winds.

What Does It All Mean?

Maclean was a Presbyterian, and he inserts tragedy and Christian motifs into his story at every turn. The footrace ahead of a rampaging fire becomes a passage through "stations of the cross." He considers the smoke jumpers' religious denominations. He imagines their conversations with God. And he compares the deaths of young men with the death of his wife. The story gets personal and more meaningful. It becomes tragedy and redemption as well as history.

Conclusion

Norman Maclean was a writer and not a historian. Yet he employs virtually every known technique of historical research and writing to make the past come alive as he tries to reconstruct and explain the events of August 5, 1949. Because of his empathy and understanding, the story of a footrace by young men against fire becomes a story of life against death. And because he writes better than most historians, we are grateful for the story of a story waiting all these years to be told, discovered, and constructed.

   Task: List all the different events to be explained in this example. Then list the different kinds of explanations tested or used by Maclean in his research and writing. How does breaking an event down into several smaller events affect the kind of evidence needed to explain those events? What type of evidence did Maclean employ?

12

Interpretation

12.1 Reviewing History

Peer review—the process of having historians familiar with the topic of a work comment critically on its value—is a powerful tool for maintaining quality control among historians. Historians regularly review the work of other historians in a wide variety of historical journals and periodicals. This complex process of peer review originated in the sciences and is widely used to check on the quality of research and writing.

A book review in a scholarly journal helps keep all publishing historians honest. It informs potential readers of the merit of a particular book or historical monograph. It summarizes in brief the argument of a work of history. And it offers criticism regarding the weaknesses of the book's evidence, style of argument, or conclusions. Book reviews help other historians understand new developments in complex fields of inquiry. They can help you understand both the quality of the book under review and the debate over issues considered in that book. A book review is a powerful tool when you do not have the time or the ability to read the book itself. It tells you what one historian thinks of the work of another. Reading book reviews will deepen and strengthen your research as you try to incorporate an often vast amount of material into your work.

Bellesiles's Arming America

In 2000, historian Michael A. Bellesiles published a controversial book titled *Arming America: The Origins of a National Gun Culture* (New

York: Alfred A. Knopf, 2000). In it, he tried to show that the myth of
an armed and effective patriotic American militia ready to fight the
British at a minute's notice was not true to history. Militias were generally poorly armed, poorly trained, and ineffectively using muskets
that were inaccurate, dangerous, and useless. Few colonists possessed
guns, according to Bellesiles's reading of wills and probate records,
and not until after the Civil War did gun ownership become widespread. *Arming America* achieved enormous attention because it attacked the basis of contemporary American gun culture and by implication the National Rifle Association (the country's largest gun owner's
organization) and the assumed right to bear arms as an American founding tradition. The book won the Organization of American Historians'
prestigious Bancroft award for American history in 2000. However,
the book quickly achieved notoriety because questions were raised
about the quality of the scholarship.

There were many critical, and even hostile, reviews of Bellesiles's
book. In "Of Arms and Men: *Arming America* and Military History," in
William and Mary Quarterly, 3d ser., 59: 1 (January 2002): 217–22,
military historian Ira D. Gruber charged that Bellesiles had "undertaken
to use the past to reform the present" (217). In summarizing the book for
the reader, Gruber observed that Bellesiles had generally minimized the
importance of guns, militias, and warfare in the colonial and early national periods of American history. Poorly trained and armed militias
were never very effective at fighting, according to Bellesiles, and peace,
not war, was the normal condition of American society until 1861.

Following this brief synopsis, Gruber criticized Bellesiles's use of
evidence and his argument. Gruber claimed that Bellesiles exaggerated
the weakness and inaccuracy of muskets with respect to rifles, the role of
bayonets, and the firepower available. Regarding militias, Gruber argued that Bellesiles "uses evidence in a partial or imprecise way" (219).
Most historians, Gruber wrote, agree that the militias were not very effective as fighting forces or very well armed. But regarding the numbers
of guns per man, Bellesiles allegedly "shaped his figures to suit his argument" (220) in order to emphasize the weakness of the militias.

Peace, Gruber argued, was not at all the norm between 1607 and
1775, when there were various wars for one-third of the time. There
were also numerous examples of internal white-on-white violence in
America that Bellesiles ignored, being "inattentive to numbers and

context" (220). Gruber added that Bellesiles underestimated the number of Americans who fought in the British army during the French and Indian War (1756–1763) and generally tried to "minimize the importance of guns, militias, and war in early America" while employing a "consistently biased reading of sources" and "careless uses of evidence and context" (222).

In "Guns, Gun Culture, and Homicide: The Relationship between Firearms, the Uses of Firearms, and Interpersonal Violence," in *William and Mary Quarterly*, 3d ser., 59: 1 (January 2002): 223–40, historian Randolph Roth presented a more detailed critique, focusing largely on Bellesiles's use of probate records. These records, inventories of people's estates made after their death, included relatively few guns, according to Bellesiles, evidence that not many colonists possessed firearms. Roth analyzed these records and argued that Bellesiles "makes arithmetic mistakes" (228, 17n), "counted inaccurately" (228), and was "biased" in his estimates (230). Roth cited several historians whose analysis of probate records revealed much higher figures of gun ownership. Roth also challenged Bellesiles's claim that whites rarely assaulted each other in the antebellum era. "Those claims are false," Roth wrote, and "every tally of homicides Bellesiles reports is either misleading or wrong" (234, 235).

Bellesiles took up the *Quarterly*'s invitation to respond to these criticisms. In the same issue, he defended himself in a long essay entitled "Exploring America's Gun Culture," 241–68. Bellesiles denied Gruber's charge that he had treated guns in American culture as "superfluous." He reiterated his claim that guns were "heavy, inaccurate, required constant care, and were subject to repeated misfiring" (258). Despite Gruber's criticism, the introduction of the bayonet made muskets more useful. Bellesiles admitted that his book was "tentative in its statistics" (260). But even if some statistics were incorrect, as Gruber claimed, "I do supply footnotes giving my sources" (261). "We sometimes seem to read the evidence differently," Bellesiles concluded, and "Gruber appears to have misunderstood my discussion of the mythology of the militia" (262).

Bellesiles also responded to Roth's careful dissection of his interpretation of probate records. He conceded a few errors in his statistics, but downplayed their significance. The book "is not . . . about probate records," he noted; "it is about the growth of an American fascination with firearms." The probate records represented only a miniscule part of his evidence: "fewer than five paragraphs in a 444–page book address probate materials" (243). Bellesiles also challenged Roth's analysis of court documents relating to assaults and homicides, noting "I read some of those records differently than he" (253). Bellesiles's defense was compromised when many of his notes were destroyed in a flood of his office. Despite the various attacks on his scholarship, Bellesiles observed that the central part of his study—"the question of arms production" in early America—remained unchallenged.

> Why, if most Americans . . . owned firearms (as my critics contend), did the government devote so much effort and money to promoting the manufacture and use of firearms? Where did the guns come from if they were widely dispersed throughout the population? Does it matter that the first gun manufacturers in North America were established by the federal government in the 1790s? Why was it necessary for the new United States government to place its first arms purchase in England? What does it mean that the federal government had to buy seven thousand English gunlocks in the 1790s so that United Sates gunmakers could make that many muskets? Why did the government repeatedly report during the first seventy years of the republic that there were not enough guns made in the United States to equip even the United States army? (257)

The dispute goes on. In part, different historians do indeed read the evidence in different ways, as Bellesiles states. But what makes the argument so high-pitched is that the historical topic of guns and militias is embedded in an ongoing political debate over gun control and the constitutional right to bear arms. As long as there is political disagreement, there will be historical disagreement as well. But the political disagreement mattered to historians less than the possibility that Bellesiles might have engaged in faulty, fraudulent, and unethical research. Peer review in this case revealed that some of the historian's facts were wrong and that he selected them to fit his argument, rather than letting his argument follow from his evidence. In April 2002, Emory University, where Bellesiles taught, even launched an investigation into whether or not he had engaged in "research misconduct." Historians charged that he had cited sources that did not exist, ignored sources that did not support his thesis, misquoted his sources, and made other errors. In October 2002, Bellesiles resigned. The Bancroft Prize committee revoked his award. But whether charges of fraud discredited his overall thesis remains a matter of debate.

Task: List the issues that seem to divide Bellesiles and his critics. How might you resolve those issues? What evidence would you need? How might you revise Bellesiles's argument to fit the evidence? How can historians' political tendencies shape their interpretation of history?

12.2 Historical Revision

Can't historians finally agree on anything? Sometimes they cannot. History thrives on continuous revision of what we believe is true about the past. Historians are normally critical of the conventional wisdom on any topic and often receptive to new interpretations that contradict that wisdom. Revising the conventional wisdom is a common, and often exciting, part of doing history.

The Denmark Vesey Slave Conspiracy (1822)

Open any American history college textbook and chances are you will find mention of Denmark Vesey. Unless it is a brand-new edition, you will probably learn that he planned a major slave revolt in Charleston, South Carolina, in 1822. Vesey, a free black man who had won his freedom in a lottery, got his odd name because he had been born on the island of St. Thomas, then owned by Denmark. He was literate, a carpenter by trade, and well versed in the Bible and the Declaration of Independence. Inspired by the Haitian slave rebellion of 1791, which led to the abolition of slavery there and the establishment of the only free black republic in the world, and by the Missouri Compromise of 1820, which prohibited slavery in the northern part of the Louisiana Purchase (except for Missouri), Vesey allegedly planned a slave rebellion.

The plan was to set fire to the city of Charleston, kill all the whites, seize ships moored in Charleston Harbor, and sail off to freedom in Haiti. Had it come to pass, it could have been the largest slave revolt in American history. But an informer betrayed Vesey and the plan. One hundred and thirty-one black men were rounded up and charged with complicity in the plot. After a secret trial, with testimony from more

than thirty accused participants, Vesey and thirty-four slaves impli-
cated in the conspiracy were hanged. These events were recounted in
the official report of the trial. The conventional wisdom among most
historians since 1822 was that Vesey had indeed conspired to lead a
slave rebellion, indicative of the widespread desire for freedom by slaves
in the South. Historian Douglas R. Egerton's critically acclaimed *He
Shall Go Out Free: The Lives of Denmark Vesey* (Madison, WI: Madison House, 1999) examined and retold this gripping episode in American history.

But did the Vesey slave conspiracy really exist? In 1964, Richard C.
Wade wrote an article suggesting that historians had exaggerated the
conspiracy, which consisted of little more than "a few rumors" ("The
Vesey Plot: A Reconsideration," *Journal of Southern History* 30, [1964]:
143–60.) At a history conference held in Charleston in 2001, historian
Michael P. Johnson went a step further, arguing that the rebellion was a
hoax. Instead of a plan by blacks to kill whites—as long alleged—it
was actually a plan by whites to kill blacks, drawn up for political gain
by Charleston mayor James Hamilton Jr. Hamilton's plan, Johnson
claimed, was to invent—and then "uncover"—a slave rebellion conspiracy, publicize its potential horrors, and blame the governor for failing to act. In the process, Hamilton hoped to advance his own career
by emerging as the savior of Charleston.

To arrive at this theory, Johnson examined not only the well-known
official report of the trial, but the original trial transcript as well. This
transcript, which was never published, exists in manuscript form in the
South Carolina state archives. The transcript differs markedly from the
official report. The official report, which was soon made available to
the public, recounts testimony by Vesey. The trial transcript, however,
makes no mention of any testimony by Vesey. The court proceedings
were held in secret, closed to the public and the press, and the transcript provides no evidence that Vesey ever even went on trial. The
transcript shows that the court, conducted by seven white magistrates,
asked witnesses questions about a conspiracy, that the witnesses did
not agree, and that they named several people besides Vesey as the
leader. Despite these discrepancies, the magistrates decided that Vesey
was the ringleader and pronounced him and others guilty. Johnson
claimed that all the witnesses were tortured and forced to testify under threat, thereby making their statements unreliable. To bolster his

argument, Johnson pointed out that after the magistrates rendered their verdict, the governor condemned the court for its "usurpation of authority, and a violation of Law." So did the governor's brother-in-law, U.S. Supreme Court justice William Johnson Jr., who wrote an article for the *Charleston Courier* attacking the court for its many irregularities. But the executions went forward and Mayor Hamilton, who claimed he had rescued Charleston from a threatened black slave revolt, was elected to Congress and then in 1830 to the governorship.

Several scholars promptly challenged Michael Johnson's revisionist account. They supported the conventional wisdom that there really was a slave conspiracy in Charleston. Historian Douglas Egerton and others argued that the torture and threats inflicted on the witnesses does not necessarily mean their testimony was untrue. Another pointed out that Johnson had based his argument entirely on the trial transcript in the state archives, ignoring letters and other evidence that there was a slave conspiracy. On the other hand, some scholars praised Johnson's detective work and challenged his critics. "The truly daunting aspect of [his] extraordinary tour de force," wrote Philip Morgan, ". . . is the complicity of historians in accepting the corrupt verdict of a kangaroo court."

Ultimately, the controversy over the Vesey conspiracy may be less a matter of fact than of interpretation. As historian Thomas J. Davis observed, "in the Vesey affair, as elsewhere, the conspiracy charge and criticism may too easily distract the historian from inquiring into more fundamental questions. The historian's conspiracy question is not usually about conspiracy, not legally. The trial courts and legal system of the day answered the legal question. Was there really a conspiracy?— meaning credible plans for an insurrection when there was no insurrection? Were there plans? If so, were the plans credible? The questions return to perception."

Johnson published an article based on his findings in *William and Mary Quarterly*, the leading scholarly journal of early American history (Michael P. Johnson, "Denmark Vesey and His Co-Conspirators," *William and Mary Quarterly*, 3d ser., 58 [October 2001]: 915–76). His critics responded in the following issue ("Forum: The Making of a Slave Conspiracy. Part 2," *William and Mary Quarterly*, 3d ser., 59 [January 2002]: 135–216). As a result of Johnson's article and the ensuing historical debate, textbooks will likely be revised in the coming years.

The furor over the Vesey affair shows no signs of abating and has achieved attention beyond the usual circle of historians. After many years of lobbying by black leaders, the city of Charleston recently approved construction of a monument to honor Denmark Vesey as a freedom fighter. A group of local whites opposed the monument because Vesey had promoted "genocide." Now it is not clear what role Vesey actually played in the affair. Was he a rebel who planned a slave revolt? Or was he simply the victim of a white supremacist plot? The questions remain unanswered for the moment.

The interested reader may find the story summarized in brief by Jon Wiener, "Denmark Vesey: A New Verdict," *Nation*, March 11, 2002, 21–24. The more interested reader will want to turn to *William and Mary Quarterly* or even the South Carolina state archives.

Task: Design an imaginary research trip for yourself to South Carolina to decide whether Johnson or his critics are right. What kind of evidence would you look for? How could you prove your case?

12.3 Historiography

Historiography is a powerful tool to help you understand the context of your own work. What is historiography? Literally the word means the study of the writing of history. Historians generally use the term *historiography* to mean the history of how historians have dealt with a particular topic. In historiography, revision is a normal part of doing history—it is the ongoing debate by historians that reveals how views of the past have changed over time. Historians regularly read and criticize the work of their predecessors, testing that work against new evidence and new interpretations, seeing things from a different angle of vision, then revising previous interpretations to produce their own. The conventional wisdom of one generation of historians becomes the revisionism of another generation. When many historians begin to revise their view of a complex series of past events, we speak of *revisionism*. Historical revisionism then may become the new conventional wisdom, subject to future revision, and so on.

In your own work, you should write a brief section on historiography for each of your papers. Historiography is really the only tool that can help you place your own work in the context of other historians and judge its originality as a contribution to knowledge.

World War II

The historiographic battle over the history of World War II (1939–1945)—the epic conflict of the twentieth century—often seems as bitterly contested as the war itself. Those who fought and won that war on the Allied side, including the United States, Soviet Union, and Britain, have one version of events. Those who lost—Germany, Japan, and Italy—have another. Even among the Allies, national histories are often in conflict. The "official" histories began even during the war and continue to proliferate. Unofficial historians contest these histories. Nations apologize, or not, for what they did during the war. Historians argue about the origins of the war, collaboration and resistance, the outcome of particular battles, and the moral issues of war crimes and financial support for the enemy. The battle for history goes on.

Historiography generally changes over time because new generations of historians either discover new evidence or develop new interpretations because of changing times and perspectives. In the case of World War II, the historiography of intelligence developed out of new evidence, and the historiography of the atomic bomb because of changing times.

How much did intelligence matter? Code breaking and intelligence became an area of controversy among historians only because of new evidence. Until 1974, few knew that the British and the Americans had broken the German and Japanese military codes and were regularly reading enemy communications "traffic," code-named "Ultra" for the Germans and "Magic" for the Japanese. But in 1974, the thirty-year limits imposed by the British Official Secrets Act began to expire and wartime code breakers began to tell their story in memoirs and interviews. Thousands of British scholars and cryptographers had worked secretly at Bletchley Park, north of London, deciphering the languages of the German Enigma machine, which set and changed codes daily. Their stories of breaking enemy codes provided a wealth of new information that historians could use to reinterpret many aspects of the war. Thousands of decoded enemy battle plans were published and analyzed by historians.

Knowing enemy plans in advance of a battle clearly provides a significant advantage. But how much of an advantage? New evidence

showed that British prime minister Winston Churchill shared Ultra decoded information with Soviet leader Joseph Stalin in advance of the
German invasion of the Soviet Union in 1941, but Stalin ignored it.
Did U.S. president Franklin D. Roosevelt know in advance that the
Japanese were going to attack Pearl Harbor? Did Churchill know in
advance that the Germans were going to bomb Coventry? Did they
protect such secrets simply in order to prevent the enemy from knowing that their codes were broken? How important were decoded enemy
intelligence reports in battles where thousands of men and machines
clashed? The answers to such questions have created a veritable industry of books on intelligence and espionage during World War II, along
with an army of critics who argue that men, weapons, and industrial
materials won the war, not intelligence.

New evidence about intelligence during World War II gave historians access to previously secret evidence that was significant in understanding the actions of wartime leaders and the success or failure of
entire armies and navies in battle. From 1974 on, no historian could
ignore the history of intelligence in writing a history of any aspect of
the war.

*Why did the United States decide to drop two atomic bombs on Japa-
nese cities?* The decision to use the atomic bomb on Hiroshima and
Nagasaki in August 1945 was particularly controversial. Historians
began to revise and rewrite the history of the atomic bomb not so much
because of new evidence as because of a changing political climate
during the Cold War.

The conventional wisdom among historians after World War II followed the official history of the Manhattan Project to build the atomic
bomb. That is, the decision by U.S. president Harry S. Truman to use
the atomic bomb was required to compel Japan to surrender and thereby
save countless American and Japanese lives in the planned invasion of
the Japanese homeland. After years of effort, scientists secretly deto-
nated the first plutonium bomb at Alamgordo, New Mexico, on July
16, 1945. This unpublished test showed that the bomb worked: the $2
billion project was a success. But should the bomb be used on Japan?
Some scientists urged in 1945 that a public test of the devastating
weapon, with invited Japanese visitors, would lead Japan to surrender.
But others, argued that even if successful, such a test would only impress the Japanese with America's apparent unwillingness to use the

bomb against them; therefore, the only course for compelling Japan to surrender and ending the long, bloody war in the Pacific was to drop the bomb directly on Japan.

In the 1960s, the conventional wisdom gave way to revisionism among many scholars. A new generation of historians argued that the bombs were not really needed to insure the surrender of an already destroyed Japan, but were used instead as a form of "atomic diplomacy" intended to impress Stalin at the outset of the Cold War. In his book *Atomic Diplomacy* (New York: Simon and Schuster, 1965), Gar Alperovitz argued that the Soviet Union, not Japan, was President Truman's real target when he decided to use the bomb. Herbert Feis promptly responded with a defense of the conventional view in his book *The Atomic Bomb and the End of World War II* (Princeton: Princeton University Press, 1966). A decade later, Martin Sherwin provided a more balanced view in his *A World Destroyed: The Atomic Bomb and the Grand Alliance* (New York: Knopf, 1975). The debate continues.

What shaped the debate over the use of the atomic bomb was not so much new evidence, but a new context. In 1945, the Soviet Union and the United States were allies in the war against Japan. The Soviet Union had declared war on Japan a few days after American bombs dropped on Hiroshima and Nagasaki. But after 1945, the Soviet Union and the United States became adversaries in a new Cold War that included a race to build and deploy nuclear weapons and missiles. The United States developed secret war plans to drop atomic and then hydrogen bombs on Soviet cities, and the Soviet Union developed similar plans against the United States. The Cold War turned hot in Korea (1950–1953).

Historians therefore began to reinterpret the events of 1945 in the context of a much later Cold War. The fact that Truman had warned Stalin at the Potsdam conference in July 1945 of a powerful, new weapon in the hands of the United States was well known. The American president spoke of a "weapon of unusual destructive force" (Stalin's spies were already well informed about the Manhattan Project). Stalin said only that he was glad the weapon would be used against Japan. Now, in the 1960s, that well-known meeting became for "revisionist" historians evidence that Truman intended to drop the bomb not simply to end the war with Japan, but to impress Stalin with America's new nuclear power. It would also give the United States much greater authority in securing the peace, negotiating terms, and rebuilding Japan. Other evidence also seemed to fit such an interpretation. The times had changed, and so had historians. They divided between those who still believed that the bomb was dropped to end the war and save American lives, and those who believed that dropping the bomb was part of the Cold War, as well as part of the end of World War II. The entire debate became public in 1995 when the Smithsonian Museum in Washington, D.C., launched a fifty-year anniversary exhibit of the B-29 bomber *Enola Gay*, which had dropped the first bomb on Hiroshima. Revisionist historians wrote the script for the exhibit, criticizing use of the bomb. World War II veterans were outraged, and the exhibit was substantially modified to avoid further controversy.

The examples of military intelligence and the decision to drop the atomic bomb during World War II illustrate that historiography changes over time both because of new evidence and because of new interpretation. Both evidence and interpretation are critical tools for the historian. But neither new evidence or new interpretations will put an end to the historical arguments that make up historiography.

The historiography of World War II is enormous and controversial. The interested reader might well begin by looking at the brief historiographic survey by military historian John Keegan, *The Battle for History: Re-fighting World War II* (New York: Vintage Books, 1995).

Task: Make sure to include a section on historiography in your next paper. What are the arguments? On what issues do historians disagree? Which revisions in historiography are based on new evidence? On new interpretation? How does your own argument fit into the historiographical debate on your topic? Are you making a contribution to the study of your topic that will interest other historians?

12.4 Women's History: The Leo Frank Case

Women's history is one of the most significant developments in the historical profession since World War II. The discipline of history had been traditionally a male preserve, with men often writing about men in male-dominated language. Male historians tended to focus on male-dominated domains, such as war, politics, and industry, and treated men as the motive force in history. Prompted by the emergence of the feminist movement in the 1960s and 1970s, an increasing number of women began to enter the historical profession. They challenged historians of both genders to study new aspects of history previously neglected—marriage, sexual relations, motherhood, sisterhood, working women, the legal status of women, property and inheritance, the women's movement itself, and the struggle for female suffrage. By the late twentieth century, women's history came of age. No longer was it possible for male historians to ignore or deny the significance of women in history. Women were increasingly important both as historians and as the subject of historical study.

Gender perspectives cast old issues in a new light and revised traditional approaches to the study of the past. Women's history flourished on the basis of both new evidence and a new perspective. By considering women and the issues of gender, historians could achieve a more complete picture of historical events.

The Leo Frank case provides a fascinating example of how the perspective of women's history provides a tool that can help us understand a complex historical event in new ways. In the early 1900s, Leo Frank was supervisor of the National Pencil Factory in Atlanta, Georgia. As a Jew raised in the North, he stood out in the largely Protestant South. In 1913, a thirteen-year-old white girl named Mary Phagan, who worked in the factory, was raped and murdered. Frank was accused of the crime and arrested. Both anti-Semitism and racism flourished in the growing South in the early twentieth century. The population of Atlanta had quadrupled between 1880 and 1910 as new people flocked to the city and its factories. Ironically, Jim Conley, a black custodian at the factory with a record of prior arrests, was suspected of the murder, but was absolved by the prosecutor, the jury, and public opinion eager to demonize a wealthy, white "Yankee Jew."

Frank's trial lasted four months. Although there was little evidence, a jury convicted him of the crime and sentenced him to death. Frank's lawyers appealed the decision all the way to the United States Supreme Court, which in April 1915 rejected the appeal. But the governor of Georgia then commuted Frank's death sentence. On August 16, 1915, a mob broke into the work farm where Frank was being held. They seized him and lynched him for a crime he had not committed. (Frank was posthumously declared innocent in 1985 by another governor of Georgia.)

Why had a southern mob and southern public opinion condemned a Jewish factory supervisor and ignored a black man who might well have committed the crime? For decades, historians viewed the case as a key example of how industrialization and urbanization of the agrarian South had unleashed dark forces of anti-Semitism and anticapitalism that pitted rural populism against urban progressivism. In 1966, as the civil rights movement gathered force, historian Leonard Dinnerstein, in *The Leo Frank Case* (Athens: University of Georgia Press), looked at Frank in terms of his race (white), religion (Jewish), background (northern), and class (middle/upper). Dinnerstein produced a thorough study of the rape and murder, the legal response, and the popular outrage against Frank's alleged crime and lynching. Dinnerstein examined all the evidence in the case and emphasized that Frank was convicted by a southern populist culture that hated him as a Yankee, an employer, and a Jew.

"Although the newspapers devoted a great deal of space to the murder they did not sufficiently explain why the police and the populace could so easily accept the indictment against Frank. To understand this more fully, an examination of the social milieu in which the case unfolded is necessary. The keynote to much of Southern society was a commitment to tradition and an opposition to change. The Southern heritage, moreover had nurtured a strong in-group loyalty which at times manifested itself as a paranoiac suspicion of outsiders. Leo Frank as a Northerner, an industrialist, and a Jew represented everything alien to that culture." (Dinnerstein, *The Leo Frank Case*, 32)

In 1991, women's historian Nancy MacLean, in an article entitled "The Leo Frank Case Reconsidered: Gender and Sexual Politics in the Making of Reactionary Populism" (*Journal of American History* 78: 3 [December 1991], 917–48), reconsidered the case from the perspective of gender, rather than race, religion, and class. She focused on the rape as well as on the murder of Mary Phagan, who to many symbolized the "flower of southern womanhood." MacLean examined the possibility that Phagan may have been sexually active—a possibility most southerners at the time could not accept. She argued that "the furor over gender relations and sexuality fueled class hostilities and anti-Semitism" (920) in reactionary populism, a form of anti-elitism that stimulated the emergence of the second Ku Klux Klan in the South.

MacLean focused less on Frank and more on Phagan as an attractive young female worker, a member of the First Christian Bible School, and a person on her way to attend a Confederate Memorial Day parade when she was murdered. She was a perfect symbol capable of uniting a broad variety of social grievances and resentments.

"Gender analysis thus opens a new window on the Frank case and the social order that produced it. Through this window, we see more clearly how change and contestation, not stasis and consensus, constituted the very essence of early twentieth-century southern history. Economic development acted as a solvent on older relations of power and authority—between men and women and between parents and children as well as between workers and employers and blacks and whites. The dissolution of the older sexual order produced losses as well as gains. The popular anxieties and resentments thereby created proved multivalent; they made class hostilities at once more volatile and more amenable to reactionary resolution. To observe these operations in the Frank case is to gain insight into the processes by which protean concerns about the family and sexuality may help tame and redirect popular opposition to a dominant social order. The inclusion of gender as a category of analysis is thus not an optional flourish, but a vital tool to uncover elements upon which both mobilization and outcome hinged." (Maclean, 921)

MacLean did not deny the conventional wisdom of the Leo Frank case, but by examining it through the lens of women's history, she gave it new perspective and new meaning, emphasizing how different groups in southern society viewed the roles of women in a rapidly changing world. She emphasized Mary Phagan as much as Leo Frank. She looked at male control of females, the anxiety about young women's sexual activity, and the sexual power of employers over employees. She looked beyond anti-Semitism and class conflict to explore how gender roles and sexual jealousies helped create the fervor and hysteria that led to Frank's lynching. She showed how a case of a female sexual victim played into the hands of a conservative populism enraged by Yankee employers, Jewish success, and urban unrest. Women's history is thus a vital tool, providing historians with a valuable perspective for understanding and reinterpreting the past.

Tasks: Reread the paragraphs on the Leo Frank case by Dinnerstein in 1966 and MacLean in 1991. What similarities and differences do you see in how they approach the case? How does a women's history perspective change your view of what happened? Consider another historical event or case with which you are familiar. Can you make it look different by considering issues of gender that may have been ignored by the conventional wisdom? Are there examples of women who have been ignored? Can you enrich your own understanding by looking at events from the point of view of women, as well as men?

13

Speculation

13.1 Historical Speculation

Speculation means coming to a conclusion without sufficient evidence. But speculation can often be a helpful tool when deepening our understanding of the context or background of events or individuals. When does a historian have the right to speculate about the past without any direct evidence? Most historians will refuse to do this. Some will speculate, often with imaginative and creative results. In general, however, you should avoid speculation, since your instructor is unlikely to share your creative impulses about the truth. If you must speculate, say clearly that you are doing so.

Will the Real Martin Guerre Please Get an Identity?

Consider the case of historian Natalie Zemon Davis's prize-winning book on sixteenth-century France, *The Return of Martin Guerre* (Cambridge, MA: Harvard University Press, 1983). Certain facts about the story of Martin Guerre are known and accepted. Guerre lived with his wife Bertrande in the Basque village of Artigat in the mountains between France and Spain. In 1548, he left Artigat to become a soldier. When Guerre failed to return over the next eight years, villagers assumed he had died. Then, in 1556, a man appeared in Artigat claiming to be Guerre. Bertrande accepted him into her bed as her rightful husband. But was he? Or was he an impostor named Arnaud du Tilh? Villagers were not sure. Over the next three years, tensions mounted between Guerre/du Tilh and Guerre's uncle, and when Bertrande and her alleged husband tried to claim an inheritance, many villagers became suspicious. A trial resulted at which many villagers testified, about half claiming the man was Guerre and half claiming he was an impostor.

The Return of Martin Guerre is a gripping story, and Davis is a brilliant and widely recognized historian. But she peppers the pages of her book with speculation. Consider the following statements [italics mine]:

- "The economic link of Artigat with nearby villages and burgs *would have been* apparent to the Daguerres at once" (10)—but was it?
- "Sanxi's wife *probably* continued to carry baskets of grain on her head" (14)—but did she?
- "The marriage contract of Bertrande and Martin has not survived but *we can assume* its content from numerous others that have" (17)—but can we?
- "The couple *must have* consulted a local wise woman more than once" (21)—but did they?
- "Among other things, *so one must surmise*, they decided to make the invented marriage last" (46)—why must one surmise this? On what evidence?
- On Protestantism: "*It is possible, even probable*, that the new Martin and Bertrande de Rols were becoming interested in the new religion" (48)—why is it possible or even probable?
- "They *must have been* among the one hundred and eighty witnesses heard before the case was through" (49)—but were they?
- "His two unmarried sisters *probably* moved back in with him, as would be expected in Basque custom" (51)—but did they?
- "The consuls of Artigat *undoubtedly* discussed the matter of Martin Guerre at many meetings in the spring and summer of 1559" (55)—but did they discuss the matter at all? If so, what records exist?

And on it goes. Other historians took Davis to task for basing much of her history of the Martin Guerre story on a continuous series of *speculations*—informed as they were by her vast knowledge of time and place—rather than on the trial transcripts, court proceedings, church records, and other evidence. That evidence simply does not support her conclusion that the "new" Martin Guerre and his wife, Bertrande, conspired to deceive the court with an invented marriage. But she uses the tool of speculation to paint a rich portrait of village life in sixteenth-century France.

Speculation is easier when one assumes that facts exist only in the mind of the historian or as words in the text. The postmodern impulse is to tell marvelous stories about the past that might be true or are as close to the truth as we are likely to get. One history is as good as another, some post-modernists say. But can the historian imaginatively reconstruct the past on the basis of context but not text, imagination but not evidence? Most historians think not. Speculation is more in the realm of fiction than of fact, even when we recognize that the lines are often blurred and that the historian constructs, as well as discovers, the historical truth.

For a substantial critique of *The Return of Martin Guerre*, see Robert Finlay, "The Refashioning of Martin Guerre," *American Historical Review* 93 (June 1988): 552–71. Natalie Davis responded with her article "On the Lame" in the same issue, 572–603.

Task: Make a list of all the different kinds of evidence you might use to prove your own identity. What are the problems with each item in terms of making a persuasive case that you know who you are and can prove it? How would you go about proving or disproving another person's identity? How would this evidence differ from that available in the sixteenth century?

13.2 History as Fiction

Historical fiction can often be solidly grounded in the facts and the sources. Such novels as *Burr* by Gore Vidal and *Cold Harbor* by Charles Frazier vividly capture and re-create distant eras and historical figures. But imagined situations and characters are fiction, not fact. History depends on being a nonfictional enterprise. May a historian legitimately introduce a fictional account into a work of history? Most historians emphatically think not. Yet the tendency to do so may be strong, even among professional historians. Fiction can make fact more colorful, more dramatic, more meaningful, more plausible, more entertaining, and more convincing. But it is still fiction. What happens when a historian introduces a fiction into an account without footnoting any source or informing the reader that what is on the page is a useful fiction, not an accurate historical account?

The Soldier Who Never Was

In his book *Dead Certainties (Unwarranted Speculations)* (New York: Vintage, 1992), eminent historian Simon Schama introduces his story of British general James Wolfe during the French and Indian War with the following dramatic account (3, 5–6):

> *"Anse du Foulon, Quebec, four a.m., September 13, 1759*
>
> Twas the darkness that did the trick, black as tar, that and the silence, though how the men contriv'd to clamber their way up the cliff with their musket and seventy rounds on their backs, I'm sure I don't know even though I saw it with my own eyes and did it myself before very long. We stood hushed on the muddy shore of the river, peering up at the volunteers. They looked like a pack of lizards unloosd on the rocks, though not so nimble, bellies hugging the cliff and their rumps wiggling with effort. We couldn't see much of 'em for they disappeared now and then into the clumps of witherd cedar and spruce that hung on the side of the hill. But we could feel the squirming, pulling labour of it all. . . . I had no sooner got to the very top and was rejoicing and taking good care not to look down behind me when our men gathered together amidst the tamaracks and the spruce. Before us were a group of tents, white in the first thin light of the coming dawn, and of a sudden a commotion and shouting broke forth. A Frenchy officer came flying out in his nightshirt as we loosd off our first rounds and sent them running across the open fields towards the town leaving a few of their company shot or stuck with our bayonets wearing that surprisd look on their face as they lay there amidst the pine needles and brown grass."

And so on and so on. This gripping firsthand account of scaling a cliff and encountering surprised French troops at Quebec is bold, graphic—and totally imagined by the historian. It is a work of fiction. There is no historical British soldier, no memoir, no document, no footnote, no source. If alert readers make their way to the end of the book, they discover a remarkable afterword in which Schama, the historian, tells us how he is doing history here:

> Though these stories may at times appear to observe the discursive conventions of history, they are in fact historical novellas, since some passages (the soldier with Wolfe's army, for example)

> are pure inventions, based, however, on what documents suggest. This is not to say, I should emphasize, that I scorn the boundary between fact and fiction. It is merely to imply that even in the most austere scholarly report from the archives, the inventive faculty—selecting, pruning, editing, commenting, interpreting, delivering judgments— is in full play. . . . Claims for historical knowledge must always be fatally circumscribed by the character and prejudices of its narrator. (Schama, 322)

Schama goes on to a further disclaimer, observing that "this book is a work of the imagination that chronicles historical events." The soldier's description of the Battle of Quebec is "purely imagined fiction" that has been "constructed from a number of contemporary documents" (Schama, 327).

Schama probably used an actual document, the journal of Captain John Knox about his campaigns in North America in 1757–1760, to construct his fictional account. Knox wrote that "this grand enterprise was conducted and executed with great good order and discretion; as fast as we landed, the boats put off for re-enforcements. . . . We lost no time here, but clambered up one of the steepest precipices that can be conceived, being almost a perpendicular, and of an incredible height. As soon as we gained the summit all was quiet, and not a shot was heard. . . . The general then detached the light troops to our left to rout the enemy from their battery, and to disable their guns, except they could be rendered serviceable to the party who were to remain there; and this service was soon performed." (See John Knox, *An Historical Journal of the Campaigns in North America for the Years 1757, 1758, 1759, and 1760*, ed. Arthur G. Doughty [Toronto: Champlain Society, 1914–1916], vol. 2, 94–101.)

Why didn't Schama simply quote from Knox's real account? Probably he felt that the real account was too dull and nonspecific for his purposes, with the language of a report from an officer to his commander. It was much more fun to imagine the dramatic than to quote the prosaic.

So the question becomes: when historians make up stories as imagined fictions, are they doing history? They probably are not. Schama is brilliantly re-creating a historical event with a nonexistent participant whose account is based on unnamed and uncited sources. Is it dramatic? Yes. Is it well informed by historical evidence? Probably. Is it good history? No.

Schama has written many fine works of history. *Dead Certainties* is not one of them, although I imagine he had great fun speculating and imagining what might well have happened. History students have no such license except in a creative fiction class.

Task: Compare the accounts of Knox and Schama's imagined soldier. What does the fictional account add to the story? Was it necessary? Is it justified? How might the urge to tell a good story distort the truth?

13.3 Conspiracies

Speculation can lead historians to develop theories and ideas that help explain the past. Conspiracy theories especially have long been popular among general readers and students. Historians treat them skeptically: like all theories, they must be based on evidence and reality. Two of the most widely studied conspiracy theories in American history focus on the assassination of President Abraham Lincoln in 1865 and the assassination of President John F. Kennedy in 1963. Who really killed Lincoln? Who killed Kennedy? Was it a lone gunman acting independently or a group of individuals secretly conspiring together? Behind every controversial event seems to lurk a hidden plot, a clandestine plan designed by some fiendish group. Rather than advance wild-eyed theories—as film director Oliver Stone did in his 1990 movie *JFK*, which relied heavily on discredited rumors—historians examine the evidence to determine what happened in a specific event, who was involved in it, and whether a conspiracy in fact existed.

Who Really Really Killed Lincoln?

On April 14, 1865, five days after the South surrendered, a well-known actor and southern patriot named John Wilkes Booth climbed into President Lincoln's box seat at Ford's Theater in Washington, D.C., and shot him with a small pistol. Booth then leaped to the stage, injuring his leg, limped from the theater, got on a horse, and rode off in the night to southern Virginia, despite a number of federal patrols and closed escape routes. A doctor named Samuel Mudd treated his broken leg. A few days later Booth was cornered by federal troops in a Virginia barn and shot. Sergeant Boston Corbett most likely killed him. Booth's body was delivered to the Washington Arsenal, where it was secretly buried. Although Booth fired the gun that killed Lincoln, he did not act alone. Others had helped plan the assassination, including George Atzerodt, David Herold, Lewis Powell, Michael O'Laughlen, and Mary Surratt. They were quickly tried and convicted by a military tribunal and then hanged. The tribunal gave long prison sentences to Mudd, Ed Spangler, and Samuel Arnold, who were all pardoned by President Andrew Johnson in 1869. Mary Surratt's son John received a civil trial in 1867, but got off because of a hung jury, and spent his days giving lectures about his mother and the assassination.

Such are the bare facts. But over the years these facts have come under scrutiny again and again in an effort to find deeper conspiracies that might have been behind the assassination. There was speculation immediately that Vice President Andrew Johnson was in on the plot because he succeeded to the presidency. There were rumors that Booth did not die, but had been sighted in Mexico, Italy, Turkey, China, and other parts of the world. In 1907, Finis L. Bates in his book *The Escape and Suicide of John Wilkes Booth* claimed that Booth had turned up as a drifter in Texas and Oklahoma before killing himself. The entrepreneurial Bates made a tidy sum renting "Booth's" mummified remains to carnivals for exhibition on into the 1930s.

As time went on, the conspiracy theories got bigger and better. Otto Eisenschiml, in his two books *Why Was Lincoln Murdered?* (Boston: Little, Brown, 1937) and *The Shadow of Lincoln's Death* (New York: Wilfred Funk, 1940), suggested that Secretary of War Edwin Stanton had masterminded the plot. After all, he asked, did not Stanton keep General Ulysses S. Grant from attending Ford's Theater that night? And why did Stanton not discipline the guard in Lincoln's box for neglect of duty? Others argued that the head of the National Detective Police, Lafayette Baker, or even Secretary of State William Seward (who was himself badly wounded in another attack) were involved.

In 1977, David Balsiger and Charles Sellier produced a book and movie, entitled *The Lincoln Conspiracy*, in which they claimed that Booth was involved in a number of broad conspiracies by Maryland planters, Confederate secret service agents in Canada, northern businessmen speculating on the cotton market, and radical Republicans wishing for a more brutal occupation of the defeated South under Reconstruction.

The most recent conspiracy theory involves the Confederate secret service, operating out of Montreal and other Canadian cities. In their book *Come Retribution: The Confederate Secret Service and the Assassination of Lincoln* (1988), William Tidwell, David Gaddy, and James Hall provide a wealth of circumstantial evidence that links Booth to shadowy agents of the Confederacy and to Confederate president Jefferson Davis personally. Didn't Booth smuggle quinine into the Confederacy from the North? Wasn't he in Montreal at the same hotel with Confederate agents in late 1864? Didn't he tell someone he knew the Confederate ciphers and codes? Tidwell and Gaddy both worked for the Central Intelligence Agency. They knew a good intelligence operation when they saw one, and this, they believed, was it.

Conspiracy theorists love assassination. They contend that a lone individual never could have carried out an assassination without a plot and lots of help. Every shred of evidence, the more circumstantial the better, becomes grist for the mill of conspiracy. The Lincoln assassination presents a superb example. After all, there was a conspiracy of sorts, as Booth acted in concert with several companions, one of whom assaulted Seward the same night. But how extensive was the conspiracy? Was anyone else—especially higher-ups or prominent individuals—involved? Here the trail grows cold as the evidence becomes murkier and murkier. Thus the argument goes on and on without end. The case is never closed.

The Kennedy assassination is even murkier. Whereas no one doubts that Booth shot Lincoln, some dispute whether Lee Harvey Oswald actually shot Kennedy on November 22, 1963. Claims of additional gunmen—one lurking behind the mysterious "grassy knoll"—surfaced almost immediately, and conspiracy theorists have pointed the finger at numerous suspects who presumably wanted Kennedy dead, such as white supremacist extremists, Cuban leader Fidel Castro, and organized crime figures. Lack of evidence has never stopped people from speculating about who might have been involved in the Kennedy assassination, and the mystery has fueled an entire industry of books and movies (including Stone's *JFK*).

Conspiracy is not so much a tool as a theory. Conspiracy theories are often faulty explanations, usually based on highly selective and sometimes discredited evidence. You should avoid assuming a conspiracy theory unless you have hard evidence to back it up. The best tool for testing conspiracy theories is evidence. Historians consider every piece of evidence to determine if there are grounds for a conspiracy.

For a good introduction to the Lincoln assassination and its conspiracy theories, see Thomas R. Turner, *The Assassination of Abraham Lincoln* (Malabar, FL: Krieger, 1999). On the Kennedy assassination, see Gerald L. Posner, *Case Closed: Lee Harvey Oswald and the Assassination of JFK* (New York: Doubleday, 1994).

Task: Dream up a conspiracy theory for some historical event of your own choosing. Then make a list of evidence that might support or contradict that theory. Is there sufficient evidence to prove that theory? To disprove it? Why do you think conspiracy theories are so popular?

13.4 Forgeries and Facsimiles

Conspiracy theories are one thing, outright fraud and forgeries are another. How do we know if something is genuine? How can we tell if a document or image in front of us is authentic? Could someone have fooled us by creating or copying a bogus document? History is replete with rogues who have forged and copied documents and images for fun and profit. A forgery is a document or image that pretends to be something it is not. A facsimile is a copy of a document or image that claims to be the original. Your best tool for detecting a forgery or a facsimile is your critical and skeptical approach to all historical sources.

Here are just a few examples:

Is a Document Genuine?

In the nineteenth century, a man named Robert Spring (born 1813 in England) emigrated to America and opened a book shop in Philadelphia. He soon found he could make more money forging documents associated with George Washington. He used a goose quill pen and mixed his own aged ink to forge Washington letters on paper that he cut out of the blank pages of old books. He then stained the paper with coffee grounds to make it appear even older and more authentic. He copied Washington's signature. His documents were usually very short

Illustration 13.1   **Alexander Hamilton's Commission Letter as Treasury Secretary**

A commission letter from George Washington to Alexander Hamilton: Is it authentic, or is it a forgery? How can you tell? (*Hamilton Papers, Library of Congress*)

(a pass through the army lines, for example), and he changed individual names every time he wanted to sell another forgery. To this day, forged Washington documents turn up all over the world several times a year. The official editors of Washington's papers at the University of Virginia have collected over 150 Spring forgeries of Washington documents signed by him. How can you detect a forgery or authenticate a document? Detection and authentication are difficult. Many documents can only be authenticated by using microscopes, by examining watermarks in the paper, and by chemically testing ink and paper.

Is a Collection of Documents Authentic?

In 1945, historians became excited about the appearance of a beautifully bound set of three volumes titled *The Horn Papers: Early Westward*

Movement on the Monongahela and Upper Ohio, 1735–1795. The papers claimed to be the diaries, maps, court records, and other artifacts of Jacob Horn and his son Christopher from about 1735 to 1795. Supposedly the papers had been found in an old chest handed down through the Horn family for many generations. Historian Julian Boyd of Princeton University, suspecting a forgery, charged that they were "complete fabrications" in the *American Historical Review*, the journal of the American Historical Association, one of the most prominent historical organizations in the country. An investigating committee turned up bad copying of known documents, examples of then unknown words and phrases ("home front," "race hatred," and "frontier spirit," for example), biographical inconsistencies, erroneous statements of fact, and internal discrepancies. The committee tested the ink and found that it dated no earlier than 1930! *The Horn Papers* became history in quite a different sense than their prankster editor (descendent W.H. Horn of Topeka, Kansas) intended. Horn never said why he forged the documents.

How Can Forgeries Influence History?

Anti-Semitism was widespread in Europe in the late nineteenth century. The *Protocols of the Elders of Zion* purported to reveal a secret meeting of Jewish elders in Prague planning to take over the world by establishing democracies, parliamentary government, banks, and other "insidious" institutions of modern society. Because the book preyed on ancient, widely held stereotypes of Jews, many Christians believed the book authentic. The model for the forgery first appeared in France in *Dialogues in Hell between Machiavelli and Montesquieu* (1864), a book critical of Emperor Napoleon III by Maurice Joly. In 1903, a right-wing Russian Orthodox monk produced a Russian-language edition for anti-Semitic groups known as the Black Hundreds. The forgery migrated to Germany after World War I with some Russian émigrés and was published in English by the anti-Semitic automobile manufacturer Henry Ford in his *Dearborn [Michigan] Independent* in 1920. Adolf Hitler mentioned the *Protocols* in his anti-Semitic screed, *Mein Kampf* (1924).

The *Protocols* did not forge any genuine document, but were a fiction masquerading as an original document. Like *The Horn Papers*, they were a complete fabrication and exposed as such in 1936. Historians have long dismissed the *Protocols* as an anti-Semitic forgery. But some people, especially in the Middle East, still believe them with deadly results. Tragically, any anti-Semitic conspiracy theory continues to find fertile soil.

Is a Newly Discovered Collection by a Well-Known Author Authentic?

Even the eminent British historian Hugh Trevor-Roper, a noted scholar of Adolf Hitler and German history, fell for this one. In 1983, the German magazine *Stern* boldly announced that it had found some sixty leather-bound volumes of Adolf Hitler's daily diary. Gerd Heidemann, a *Stern* reporter known for his interest in ex-Nazis and Nazi memorabilia, trumpeted this discovery as earthshaking. *Newsweek* ran selections from the diary. Historians sat on the edge of their chairs with eager anticipation. But careful analysis showed that the handwriting was an inept imitation of Hitler's own style, that the imitation leather did not match the elegant and real leather Hitler used at his own desk, and that all the events described in the diaries matched perfectly the entries in Max Domarus's *Hitler: Speeches and Proclamations, 1932–1945*, published in 1962–1963. In the end, the diaries turned out to have been a completely bogus creation of Konrad Kujau, a Stuttgart dealer in Nazi art and memorabilia. Trevor-Roper, who edited the diaries and vouched for their authenticity, was thoroughly embarrassed by the affair. Heidemann and Kujau served prison terms for fraud.

If It Is a Forgery, Who Is the Forger?

Demonstrating a forgery often means identifying the forger. For centuries, the famous twelfth-century *Igor Tale* has stood as the only great piece of epic poetry from medieval Russia. Critics compare it to the *Song of Roland*. Books and seminars dealing with the *Igor Tale* abound. There has long been some skepticism about the work, whose original manuscript supposedly burned in a fire in Russia in the late eighteenth century. Just recently, Harvard historian Edward Keenan has apparently discovered the man who actually forged the *Igor Tale*, a Czech Slavic scholar working in Prague in the 1820s. If Keenan's argument survives the test of peer review successfully, he will have unmasked as a forgery one of the greatest and best-known examples of Russian literature. He will have achieved something quite remarkable.

These examples suggest that historians should approach all their sources with a critical eye. Your best tools for treating sources critically are a skepticism about authenticity and a knowledge of the origins of every source: its original location, author, owner, history, and context. In other words, let's be careful out there!

Task: Choose a primary source. Who wrote it? When? Where? Why? How can you be sure? Have other historians vouched for its authenticity? Might it be a facsimile or a forgery? If so, who might have copied or forged it and why?

For Further Exploration

On forgeries and facsimiles, including the Hitler diaries, see Kenneth W. Rendell, *Forging History: The Detection of Fake Letters and Documents* (Norman: University of Oklahoma Press, 1994), especially 106–23. On other specific examples, see Dorothy Twohig on the Washington forgeries, *Provenance: The Journal of the Society of Georgia Archivists* 1 (Spring 1983): 1–13; Arthur Pierce Middleton and Douglass Adair, "The Mystery of the Horn Papers," *William and Mary Quarterly*, 3d ser., 4 (October 1947): 409–43; Norman R. Cohn, *Warrant for Genocide: The Myth of the Jewish World Conspiracy and the Protocols of the Elders of Zion* (New York: Harper and Row, 1967); B.W. Segel, *A Lie and a Libel: The History of the Protocols of the Elders of Zion*, trans. and ed. Richard S. Levey (Lincoln: University of Nebraska Press, 1995); Edward L. Keenan, *Joseph Dobrovsky and the Origins of the "Igor Tale"* (forthcoming).

13.5 Fiction as History

Some people, like Robert Spring, forged historical documents for money. Others, like the authors of the *Protocols of the Elders of Zion*, forged and fictionalized events to foment hatred. But sometimes the motivation for deception is not entirely clear. Take the case of one Benjamin Wilkomirski. In 1995, he published *Fragments: Memories of a Wartime Childhood* (New York: Schocken Books), a remarkable memoir of his childhood in the Nazi death camps during World War II.

In it, he recounted the terrible story of being a toddler rendered home-
less when the Nazis destroyed the Riga ghetto in Latvia, being separated from his family, deported to Poland, and somehow surviving
Auschwitz and other concentration camps. The book was well received
and widely reviewed as an accurate and deeply touching recollection
of the Holocaust. It was translated into twelve languages and made
into three films and a play. For three years, Wilkomirski gave lectures
and collected prizes for his memoirs. He told stories of unspeakable
horror and brutality in the camps. He cried frequently in public. He
seemed to epitomize the unspeakable cruelties inflicted on innocent
children in a world of evil.

Then in 1998, another Holocaust survivor, Daniel Ganzfried, claimed
fraud in a sensational article in the Zurich journal *Weltwoche*. Ganzfried
charged that Wilkomirski was neither Jewish nor Latvian, but actually
a Swiss Protestant named Bruno Dossekker, born on February 22, 1941,
to an unmarried couple, Yvonne Berthe Grosjean, who gave him up for
adoption, and Rudolf Zehnder. (His mother later married Walter Max
Rohr and died in 1981.) Bruno was raised by a series of foster parents,
lastly Walter and Olga Dossekker, who legally adopted him in May
1945. (They died in 1985.) He spent the entire war not in the camps of
Poland, but in Switzerland. He was simply a Swiss musician and in-
strument builder, married and the father of three children. His account
of the Holocaust was a fictional biography, a novel, but not history.

Dossekkar/Wilkomirski claimed in response that he had, in fact,
survived the harrowing experiences of Auschwitz and other concentration camps in Poland. He admitted that his Swiss documents were authentic, but claimed that, like many Holocaust orphans, he received a
new identity after the war. He said that he was born a Jew in Latvia in
early 1939 and that his Swiss identity and birth date were legal fictions. "It was always the free choice of the reader to read my book as
literature or to take it as a personal document," he added. "Nobody has
to believe me." Wilkomirski then suffered a nervous breakdown and
was hospitalized and in seclusion for some six months.

Wilkomirski claimed that he did not arrive in Switzerland until late
1947. But Ganzfried found evidence that he had moved in with his
foster parents in October 1945. When faced with such a contradiction,
Wilkomirski brushed it aside.

Was the memoir a hoax? Was Wilkomirski a conscious liar? Or was he the victim of his own delusions of the past, gleaned from other Holocaust survivors? Was he fact or fiction? He himself did not care. Only memory mattered. At one level, he claimed objectivity: "I just happen to be a historian, too." At another level, he disavowed any belief in the validity of historical records: "No matter what they say, or what they constructed—legal or not legal, half-legal papers—this is all shit for me. I know that I can trust my memory. *Basta* [*Enough!*]." No wonder high school friends remembered him as a practiced, if occasional, liar.

But Wilkomirski persisted. He claimed to be practicing "interdisciplinary therapy" so that fact and fiction were intertwined in memory and could not ever be distinguished. The Holocaust existed as historical experience because he remembered it. Memory trumped evidence. To doubt the veracity of his account would be, in his view, to doubt the Holocaust.

Wilkomirski did not deny the Holocaust. He fictionalized it. Certainly much of his book could have reflected his long-standing conversations with Holocaust survivors and his postwar visits to the camps. But even as fiction, Wilkomirski's stunning book raised questions about identity and memory in the recollection of historical experience. In fact, critics who admired the book suggested that the publisher simply reclassify it as fiction. As a work of fiction, his "memoirs" would be gripping enough. But his claim to have lived through the experience he knew only secondhand was false. He was neither historian nor primary source nor memoirist. Perhaps he was deluded by a "compelling fantasy." Perhaps he was a con man. He was, at any rate, a fiction writer posing as a nonfiction survivor, even though he himself may not have recognized the fact. Would you?

How can one tell whether a memoir or autobiography written many years after the events portrayed is fiction or nonfiction, real or imagined? If the writer believes an account is true, is it valid, even if it contradicts some known evidence? How do our later memories vary from the events we remember?

The best tool available in confronting a historical account that may be fictional is a critical approach to all memoirs and autobiographies. Understand why and under what circumstances an individual wrote a memoir. Cross-check statements against other verifiable accounts of the same events. A memoir consistent with most other accounts is probably reliable.

On the Wilkomirski affair, see Philip Gourevitch, "The Memory Thief," in *The New Yorker*, June 14, 1999: 48–68. Daniel Ganzfried's charges appeared in *Die Weltwoche*, August 27, 1998. See also Dorrit Cohn, "Fictional versus Historical Lives: Borderlines and Borderline Cases," *Journal of Narrative Technique* 19: 1 (Winter 1989): 3–24. Most recently, see Blake Eskin, *A Life in Pieces: The Making and Unmaking of Benjamin Wilkomirski* (New York: W.W. Norton, 2002).

Task: What facts in Wilkomirski's story seem most likely to be true? False? What specific circumstances made it possible for him to invent a fictional past? Write an autobiographical paragraph recounting some event or experience in your life. Write a second paragraph inventing an event or experience in your life. Try to make each as real and believable as you can. Exchange these paragraphs with another student's paragraphs and see if each of you can determine which is real and which is fictionalized. How can you tell? What clues are there? How can we know if what we read is true or not?

13.6 Film as History: Fact or Fiction?

How does film reenact, help us understand, and "get inside" a historical event? How does film distort the past by providing us with an entertaining illusion? Certainly film is a powerful tool for seeing and hearing history. It provides us with the sights and sounds of a recreated past that can have a powerful impact on us. Film can put us "there" in ways that the printed page simply can never accomplish. But it can also distort, falsify, or simply ignore historical truth. The following positive and negative examples of film and history should get you thinking about this topic.

Film Can Help the Historian Understand the Past

- *Films can help document the past.* Ken Burns is perhaps the best-known documentary filmmaker of our times. A documentary—the term itself dates back to 1935—is a work of art based on evidence and fact, generally a film or radio program. For the first documentaries in the early 1900s, many directors simply opened the camera lens and portrayed real life around them. More recently, they have tried to combine images and sounds from the past to bring us directly there. Burns has produced masterful films on Louisiana politician Huey Long, the Civil War, baseball, jazz, and the women's movement in the nineteenth century. He interviews both participants and historians on camera, reproduces old films and photographs, and lets us hear the music and sounds of a bygone era as recorded at the time. He makes history live for us in the present with loving attention to detail and historical accuracy. Documentaries aim to be true, but like any work of history are subject to bias, distortion, and interpretation.

- *Films can help us visualize the past.* The 1965 film *Dr. Zhivago*, with Omar Sharif and Julie Christie, tells the dramatic story of the Russian Revolution based on Nobel Prize winner Boris Pasternak's 1956 novel of the same name. Although based on a historical event and a specific era, there are numerous points where the film deviates from historical fact. (Even the opening scene of Zhivago's funeral is shot in Spain.) But what the movie does remarkably well—far better than a work of history could—is to convey visually the many elements of symbolism in the novel. On the printed page, Pasternak is forced to show us frost-covered windows and shattered dreams in words. The film uses visual images to give us powerful insights into love, revolution, and history. It fictionalizes the past but vividly evokes another era, thus enhancing our understanding of history.
- *Film can help us understand mental states.* In the 2001 film *A Beautiful Mind*, based on the 1998 biography by Sylvia Nasar, we see the life and mind of the tormented Nobel Prize-winning economist and mathematician John Nash. Film critics have pointed out that the movie ignores or contradicts many of the facts of Nash's life described in the biography. Props are often from the wrong decade (his wife wears espadrille shoes not popular in America until the 1970s); the Nevada atomic bomb test shown to Nash in 1953 was not held until 1955; Nash gave no Nobel speech because he was so ill at the time; mathematics is limited to a few drawings on a blackboard; and an insight into game theory is supposedly based on picking up a woman in a bar, rather than mathematics. Despite these inaccuracies and drawbacks, the film gets it right about Nash's disease, schizophrenia. The movie effectively conveys the results of insulin shock therapy and the

visual patterns seen by a mind descending into madness. The portrait of Princeton University in the 1950s is remarkably true to
life, even if some of the events are made up. The film conveys
more realistically than a history book ever could the state of Nash's
tormented mind, if not his life and work. It gets us inside his head
as no book could.

Films Can Hinder Our Understanding of the Historical Past

- *Films can be based on bad history.* The 1990 movie *JFK* by director Oliver Stone provides great entertainment and feeds the para-
  noia of movie audiences who come to the theater prepared to
  believe in a conspiracy to assassinate President John F. Kennedy
  in 1963. In this case, Stone treats the long discredited theories of
  a Dallas, Texas, assistant district attorney, Jim Garrison, as historically valid. The result is a conspiracy theory film that hints darkly
  at plots to kill President Kennedy by anti-Castro Cubans, Castro,
  the mob, and highly placed Americans in the CIA, FBI, and other
  agencies. In this case, a director takes bad history and turns it into a
  dramatic film that entertains only as a work of fiction.
- *Films can be anachronistic.* The 1998 film *Titanic* is a fictionalized love story set on the doomed ocean liner that sank on its
  maiden voyage in 1912. The ship, parts of which were rebuilt on
  a scale model, looks vivid on screen, and many scenes capture the
  splendor of the Edwardian era. And yet numerous details in the
  film are wrong. Claude Monet's painting of water lilies shown
  framed on the wall was not painted until 1923. In one scene viewers can glimpse a Roosevelt dime, which was not minted until
  1950. The crown and torch on the Statue of Liberty are shown as
  lit at night, which did not occur until the 1950s. The color photograph of a diamond would have been impossible, since no color
  photography was used at the time. The Colt 1911 pistol used by
  one of the characters was limited to military use and would have
  been quite illegal for a civilian to carry. And so on.
- *Films can be historically inaccurate.* In the 1998 film *Saving Private Ryan*, director Steven Spielberg took on the epic topic of the
  Normandy invasion of Europe in June 1944 on D-day. The first
  half hour provides one of the most gripping, horrible, realistic

views of battle ever created or replicated on film. And yet, as moving and convincing as the scene is, inaccuracies abound. The German Tiger tanks of a Panzer division used against American troops defending a bridgehead were not actually there on D-day. The village battle against the Nazi Panzer division Das Reich was also a mistake—the division was nowhere near Normandy at the time. The P-51 fighters used in the film as "tank busters" were actually used mainly for bomber escort service during the war. The antitank aircraft used at Normandy were Hawker Typhoons, and they were British, not American.

Another war movie, *The Patriot* (2000), provides a dramatic view of the American Revolution in the Carolinas. It blends fact and fiction together in a powerful way. But why are those uniforms so clean? And why does the battlefield at Cowpens look nothing like the actual battlefield? The British Union Jack flag is actually the current one, not the one used in the eighteenth century, which did not have the diagonal red cross of St. Patrick. The British never burned a church with people in it, as they do in the film. The comment "Tell me about Ohio!" uttered by one of the characters makes no sense, since Ohio was not yet either a territory or a state. The Green Dragoons in the film inexplicably wear red uniforms, when in fact they wore (guess what!) green uniforms.

Whether accurate or inaccurate, film provides a powerful tool for conveying and understanding—or misunderstanding—history. Through film, we can imagine ourselves in another time and place. We understand the past visually and aurally. Past images and sounds in a film can supplement historical texts we have read. Films can also be primary sources that tell us about the time, place, and circumstances under which they were made. They are pieces of evidence about the director, the audience, and the culture that produced them and paid to see them.

Task: Choose any film you have seen recently that involves a historical event, person, or context. Make your own list of the ways in which that film helps you understand history. Then make another list of how that same film hinders your understanding of history. Was the film accurate? Did it increase or decrease your understanding of history? What are the differences between a documentary and a historical film? What are the merits and drawbacks of each? How does each shape our view of the past?

For Further Reading

For a good recent study of the way history becomes entertainment, see Peter C. Rollins, *Hollywood as Historian*, 2d ed. (Lexington: University Press of Kentucky, 1998). A highly insightful look at the relationship between history and film is Siegfried Kracauer, *History: The Last Things Before the Last* (New York: Oxford University Press, 1969). For a fascinating grocery list of nitpicking historical mistakes in a number of historical films, see the Web site http://www.nitpickers.com/ movies/nitpicks.

14

Everyday History

14.1 Studying Ordinary People

Ordinary people, rather than extraordinary leaders and event makers, may sometimes provide a useful tool for understanding a society or culture. But how can historians study ordinary people? Who is ordinary? How do ordinary people reflect their society and their times? What sources exist to tell us about ordinary people? History today, especially social history, certainly involves the study of ordinary people, as well as "great" individuals. While we still enjoy our biographies of princesses and film stars, presidents and generals, we are equally fascinated by the lives and stories of so-called ordinary people. Most people, after all, do not so much affect history as reflect their society and their times. The problem is that ordinary people largely go unnoticed and rarely leave traces. One may read with delight, then, one account of an ordinary person who turns out to be quite extraordinary—Anna Buschler, a sixteenth-century German woman who conducted a lifelong struggle for justice within a court system run by and for men.

The Burgermeister's Daughter

Harvard historian Steven Ozment must have been elated when he discovered the court records of Anna Buschler (1496/8–1552), daughter of the burgermeister of the German town of Schwabisch Hall during the Protestant Reformation. Schwabisch Hall was an imperial city run by a council of twenty-six men drawn from the nobility and middle class of the surrounding region. As a young woman during the early 1520s, living in her father's house, Anna somehow managed to carry on two love affairs simultaneously with Erasmus Schenk, a young nobleman, and Daniel Treutwein, a cavalryman from the lower nobility. These affairs were recorded in some detail in Anna's letters to and from both men, letters found by her father in his own house and used in subsequent court proceedings. Anna worked for several years at the Schenk castle outside of town, while living in her parents' home (her mother had died in 1520). She refused to marry either of her lovers and soon became a local scandal and an embarrassment to her beleaguered father, Hermann Buschler, perhaps Hall's leading citizen.

By 1525, both Erasmus and Daniel had disappeared from Anna's life. By 1533, Erasmus, after a bout with syphilis, had married someone else and become a Lutheran. Anna now petitioned the Hall city council and the imperial supreme court for a share of her mother's inheritance and her father's estate so that she could live independently. As a dependent child and an unemployed single woman, she needed a male to represent her interests. Her father Hermann responded by petitioning the imperial ruling council for parental custody over his wayward daughter and a "mandate for surreptitious capture" so that he could bring her home after she escaped. Having retrieved Anna, Hermann kept her chained to an oak table for six months, a prisoner in her own home.

The tale that follows is bizarre. Anna succeeded in getting ever more inadequate portions of her father's money. He continued to try to disinherit her, on the grounds that she had rejected his proposed marriage arrangements in the past. After his death, in 1543, the town council ruled that she should get her fair share of the inheritance. But now her siblings took her to court. She was arrested, imprisoned, then released. The whole affair dragged on in the courts in a competition between her father's last will and testament and her parents' marriage contract, which contradicted each other. Agreements with her siblings broke down in acrimony.

In the end, Ozment concludes that Anna Buschler's story makes her an ordinary "sign of the times," but also a hero. She was able for several decades to exert her legal rights in court despite the fact that she was a woman. The Schwabisch Hall city council continued to hear her case. She mirrors in a sense the broader upheavals in German society spawned by the Reformation, religious wars, and peasant revolts. (Ozment's links with these broader trends are sometimes tenuous.) Anna Buschler was her own success story, a story "stranger than fiction" and "truer than history."

Because of the legal paper trail left by Anna Buschler's lifelong dispute with her family over her inheritance, the historian was able to turn an "average," hitherto unknown woman into a remarkable person. The conventional wisdom that women were virtually without rights in the sixteenth century is revised, at least in this case. We discover in the end through the historical evidence that an apparently ordinary person was really quite extraordinary. Examining the lives of ordinary people can be a very useful tool for historians.

For the full story of Anna Buschler and her life, see Steven Ozment, *The Burgermeister's Daughter: Scandal in a Sixteenth-century German Town* (New York: HarperCollins, 1996).

Task: Consider Anna Buschler again. What aspects of her life seem ordinary? Extraordinary? What might her life story tell us about her society? How does a biography of a generally unknown person differ from one of a famous person? What are the merits and advantages of each kind of history?

14.2 Everyone's a Historian

How does doing history resemble our everyday activities? In what sense are we all historians all the time? If so, what tools do we use in our daily round? Certainly the study of the past bears comparison with the study of our own past. Some even consider autobiography at the root of all history. Here are some random thoughts on how history is not some arcane academic enterprise, but a deep structure that underlies our own lives.

- *Memory:* You get up in the morning. In order to function, you need to remember daily routines, overdue bills, medical appointments, feeding the pets, and myriad other items in order to function at all. Alzheimer patients who have lost their memory have also lost their identity and their ability to function.
- *Evidence and records:* Did you pay that bill? Better look in your

checkbook. You should have a record of past checks written, as well as canceled checks cashed, to provide you (or the IRS) with evidence that you did or did not pay that (deductible?) bill.

- *Chronology:* Just when was that second paper due in my class? Better consult the syllabus for the course, which provides a chronology, or chronicle, of what assignments are due on what day and at what hour. (And whose birthday is it today anyway?)

- *Story:* All of us sit around the breakfast or dinner table every day and tell stories to our roommates or significant others of what we have recently (or distantly) done. Telling stories is at the root of history. We do it all the time.

- *Reading history:* Again, we do it all the time. Just consider the morning newspaper (or the Internet) and the enormous amount of historical information that we read every day. How can we possibly remember all that history? We don't. We remember selectively.

- *Research:* You are involved in an accident. Thankfully no one was hurt, but there was considerable damage. Does your insurance company cover the damage? Better research your insurance policy and see just what all that fine print you never looked at actually says. Research into your policy will help you and the insurance company negotiate a reimbursable claim.

- *Argument:* Argument is a basic part of every discourse. We want to convince our instructor that we really deserve an incomplete in the course, an extension on the paper, or an excused absence for our early departure for break. We need to convince or persuade someone else that our case is valid.

- *Maps:* You are throwing the mother of all parties. You want everyone to get there. How? Make a map of how to get to your apartment, dormitory, or home. Send it to those you have invited to the party. It will be an invaluable primary source for them.

- *Photographs:* You are spending time abroad and want a historical record of all those exotic places you just visited. How do you create that record? Perhaps with a diary, but definitely with a camera or camcorder. A photograph provides visual evidence that you really were there and had a great, or not so great, time.

- *Films:* Virtually every film you see has historical context embedded in it. Some films are based on historical events. Every film has a history of how it was made, who the stars were, how much it cost, how much it made at the box office, and what the film critics thought about its merits.

- *Events:* We live through, or witness, historical events daily, thanks to the miracle of the Internet and television worldwide news. Today's event is the Israeli attack on Palestinian towns and refugee camps in revenge for a series of suicide bombings by Palestinian terrorists. Clearly that attack has historical significance. What that significance will be, we do not yet know.

Surely by now you get the idea. The tools in the historian's toolbox can be just as useful every day in living your life as they can be in doing, or enjoying, history. You are in some sense a historian every day of your life. History can certainly give you a valuable perspective on how to live your life, even when it does not appear to be directly relevant. You know and do more history than you realize. Understanding that you do may be yet another important tool.

Task: Write down what you did yesterday. Then write down what evidence you might use to prove to a friend that you did what you did. You are doing history.

Glossary

anthropology	the study of humankind; a discipline related to history that utilizes linguistic, material, and mythological evidence to study human origins
archaeology	the recovery of material evidence for human life and culture
archive	a repository for historical documents, artifacts, or images
argument	persuasive logic that is based on premises, supported by evidence, and leads to a conclusion
artifact	an object made by humans that is of historical or archaeological interest
bias	an opinion that hinders judgment and is not based on argument or evidence; prejudice
bibliography	a list of books, articles, and unpublished manuscript and archival sources normally placed at the back of a historical monograph
biography	the life history of one particular individual, including an account of the individual's time and place
book review	a published critique of the work of one historian, normally by another historian

cartography	the study of maps
cause	something that produces, or leads to, an event, idea, or action
chromosome	a linear strand of DNA that carries and transmits genetic information
chronicle	a narrative listing of historical events in chronological order, normally by date
chronology	a listing of dates and events in the order they occurred
citation	a reference to a particular source or work
cliometrics	the quantitative study of history emphasizing numbers and mathematics
conspiracy theory	an explanation of past events that assumes a plan or plot, with or without appropriate evidence
conventional wisdom	historical knowledge that is commonly accepted until revised by historians subsequently
culture	the art, religion, literature, music, and other creations and beliefs of a society
database	electronic collection of historical sources, images, sounds, records, bibliographies, or other historical data
dissertation	a major original work of historical research and writing required for the doctor of philosophy degree in history
DNA	deoxyribonucleic acid, which contains genetic information in a cell, replicates itself, and determines hereditary characteristics; can establish identities and relationships among individuals, living or dead
document	a written source (letter, memorandum, book, article, grocery list, etc.)
draft	an unrevised piece of writing, subject to future revision until a final draft is complete

edit	to make stylistic and substantive suggestions or corrections to a manuscript or paper, to help revise
empathy	understanding another person in another time and place
evidence	material that supports an argument, normally drawn from primary sources
evolution	gradual change and progression over time
explanation	a demonstration or argument showing how or why an event occurred
facsimile	a copy of an original
fact	an established and verifiable piece of information about the past
fair use	reproduction of a copyrighted work for educational or research purposes
fiction	an imagined or invented story
file	an ordered collection of documents in an archive
footnote	an acknowledgement in the text of a source where information or interpretation was found
forgery	an invented document that falsely claims to be something it is not
genealogy	a historical record of the descent of a family or individual from ancestors; lineage or pedigree
genome	a complete set of chromosomes
hagiography	study and writing of the lives of saints; a biography that idealizes its subject
historian	one who researches evidence and tries to understand the past, often constructing a narrative, argument, or analysis of past events, ideas, or people

historical event	an occurrence in the past, selected and made significant by the historian
historicism	the belief that the meaning of history is internal, not external, to history
historiography	the study of the history of historical writings
history	the study of the past; a nonfictional account of the past
idealism	the belief that history is primarily what human beings thought or intended
index	a list of entries at the back of a book indicating on what pages something related to that entry may be found
interlibrary loan	a book, article, or manuscript copy obtained from one library for use in another library, often by photocopy, microfilm, or microfiche
interpretation	a conclusion based on evidence that gives meaning; historians may have different interpretations of the same evidence
journal	a scholarly periodical that publishes current research
law	a rule that determines, explains, or predicts a recurrent course of history
manuscript	a handwritten text; an author's printed text prior to publication
master narrative	the dominant and accepted story of past events
meme	an idea, ideology, value, or fashion that may or may not endure over time
memoir	an autobiography, an account of one's own life
memory	the recollection of the past
metahistory	an explanation of all history in terms of one factor (economics, class, civilizations, progress, freedom, great women, etc.)

microhistory	the history of a single event or community in great detail
monocausal	having one cause
monograph	a single volume or book investigating a fairly specialized historical topic
multicausal	having many causes
narrative	a modern literary-critical term for story, relating a sequence of events
note	a summary, quotation, citation, or comment written down as a record of a text, image, or sound being considered
note taking	a process whereby the historian selects from sources, and writes down, what is to be remembered and possibly used in a subsequent history
objectivity	judgment based on evidence without personal bias
on-line catalog	an indexed guide to or listing of historical sources and writing, often linked to other catalogs or Web sites
oral history	history based on oral interviews of surviving witnesses or participants
ordinary language	language in common or everyday use by most people
outline	a skeletal framework for a paper, article, book, or argument
paradigm	an accepted set of questions framed by a community of inquiry
paraphrase	to say the same thing in different words
past	what has happened until the present, not necessarily observed or recorded
peer review	the critical feedback provided by other scholars in one's field regarding one's own work; published book reviews in scholarly journals are a normal part of peer review

periodical	journal appearing at regular intervals
permissions	rights to reproduce or republish words or images owned or copyrighted by another publisher or author
philosophy of history	an analysis of the ways in which historians make assumptions, use language, frame questions, or otherwise employ theories to help explain the past
plagiarism	presenting the words or thoughts of another as if they were one's own without proper acknowledgment; a form of lying, cheating, and stealing
positivism	the nineteenth-century belief that history is a science, can test laws of human behavior, and can establish the truth about the past
postmodernism	a recent attitude toward modernity and history that minimizes or denies the external existence of truth, past, and fact except through present narrative and text
prediction	a statement of what will happen in the future
proofread	to examine a text to correct mistakes in spelling, grammar, or content; to read prior to publication or submission in order to improve
public domain	accessible to all, not protected by copyright
question	a query asked by the historian of the sources
quotation	the words of another author or person indicated in the text by quotation marks at the beginning and end of those words
quotation marks	the symbols (" ") used to signify that the words are those of another author
record	a trace of the past, normally written at the time for posterity
relativism	the belief that there is no absolute truth, only relatively true statements believed by those who make them

research paper	a limited exploration of a particular topic whose findings are based on original research in primary and secondary sources
revise	to improve by changing (1) the style and content of a piece of writing, or (2) the accepted interpretation (conventional wisdom) of a particular historical topic
revisionism	historical research and writing that contradict the conventional wisdom about a historical topic
revolution	a sudden, dramatic, and often violent change in the order of things
rough draft	a first attempt at writing, subject to future revision until a final version is completed
selectivity	choosing from among many sources of information or ideas the few that appear to be significant in some predetermined way
skepticism	being unwilling to accept anything on faith; doubt
source	(1) primary: a document, image, or artifact that provides evidence about the past provided at the time; (2) secondary: a book, article, film, or museum that displays primary sources selectively in order to interpret the past. Many sources may be both primary and secondary with respect to different entities
speculation	drawing a conclusion without the benefit of evidence or facts; imagination
summary	a short version of a text, argument, or document that conveys ideas and information in brief
table	a graphic way of showing trends, quantitative results, or other data
text	written or printed words; the body of a work distinct from preface, footnotes, appendix, or index; a textbook

textbook   a book that presents a large amount of material about a subject based upon the research and writing of many people

thesis   an argument; also shorthand for a dissertation

topic   an area or field of historical inquiry and research. A topic is not a question. Historians ask, and try to answer, different questions in order to understand a topic

world wide web   a global electronic information network accessible by computer and linking the user to databases of interest

zero-sum   in game theory, the idea that one player's gain is another player's equal loss

Selected Bibliography

Appleby, Joyce, Lynn Hunt, and Margaret Jacob. *Telling the Truth about History.* New York: W.W. Norton, 1994.

Archiving Early America: http://www.earlyamerica.com.

Aveni, Anthony. *Empires of Time: Calendars, Clocks and Cultures.* New York: Basic Books, 1989.

Bancroft, George. *History of the United States from the Discovery of the American Continent.* 9 vols. Boston: Little, Brown, 1857–66.

Bates College Web site on plagiarism: http://www.bates.edu/pubs/plagiarism.

Bede, Venerable. *Ecclesiastical History of the English People.* London: Penguin Books, 1990.

Bellesiles, Michael A. *Arming America: The Origins of a National Gun Culture.* New York: Alfred A. Knopf, 2000.

Benjamin, Jules R. *A Student's Guide to History.* Boston: Bedford Books, 1998.

Berdyaev, Nikolai. *The Meaning of History.* Translated from the Russian by George Reavey. Cleveland: Meridian, 1962 [1936].

Berlin, Isaiah. *The Hedgehog and the Fox: An Essay on Tolstoy's View of History.* New York: Mentor, 1957.

Blackmore, Susan. *The Meme Machine.* New York: Oxford University Press, 1999.

Bloch, Marc. *The Historian's Craft.* New York: Alfred A. Knopf, 1953.

Braudel, Fernand. *On History.* Chicago: University of Chicago Press, 1980.

British Library A2A Database: http://www.a2a.pro.gov.uk/.

Brodie, Richard. *The Virus of the Mind. The New Science of the Meme.* Seattle: Integral Press, 2001.

Brown, Norman O. *Life against Death.* Middletown, CT: Wesleyan University Press, 1957.

Burke, Kenneth. *The Philosophy of Literary Form.* 2d ed. Baton Rouge: Louisiana State University Press, 1967.

Butterfield, Herbert. *The Whig Interpretation of History.* London: Penguin Books, 1931.

Carr, E.H. *What Is History?* New York: Alfred A. Knopf, 1961.

Cohn, Dorrit. "Fictional versus Historical Lives: Borderlines and Borderline Cases." *Journal of Narrative Technique* 19:1 (Winter 1989): 3–24.

Collingwood, Robin G. *The Idea of History.* New York: Oxford University Press, 1943.

Costello, Paul. *World Historians and Their Goals. Twentieth-century Answers to Modernism.* Dekalb: Northern Illinois University Press, 1993.

Cowley, Robert, ed. *What If? The World's Foremost Military Historians Imagine What Might Have Been.* New York: Putnam, 1999.

Davis, Natalie Zemon. "On the Lame." *American Historical Review* 93 (June 1988): 572–603.

———. *The Return of Martin Guerre.* Cambridge, MA: Harvard University Press, 1983.

Dray, William H. *Philosophy of History.* 2d ed. Englewood Cliffs, NJ: Prentice Hall, 1993.

Eley, Geoff. *The "Goldhagen Effect": History, Memory, Nazism—Facing the German Past.* Ann Arbor: University of Michigan Press, 2001.

Eliade, Mircea. *Cosmos and History: The Myth of the Eternal Return.* New York: Harper and Row, 1959.

Evans, Richard. *In Defense of History.* New York: W.W. Norton, 1999.

Finlay, Robert. "The Refashioning of Martin Guerre." *American Historical Review* 93 (June 1988): 552–71.

Fischer, David Hackett. *Historians' Fallacies: Toward a Logic of Historical Thought.* New York: Harper and Row, 1970.

———. *Paul Revere's Ride.* New York: Oxford University Press, 1994.

Geyl, Peter. *Debates with Historians.* New York: Meridian, 1958.

Gilderhus, Mark T. *History and Historians: A Historiographical Introduction.* Upper Saddle River, NJ: Prentice Hall, 2000.

Gordon-Reed, Anne. *Thomas Jefferson and Sally Hemings: An American Controversy.* Charlottesville: University of Virginia Press, 1997.

Gray, Paul. "Other People's Words," *Smithsonian Magazine* 32:12 (March 2002): 102–3.

Hexter, J.H. *On Historians.* Cambridge, MA: Harvard University Press, 1979.

———. *The History Primer.* New York: Basic Books, 1971.

Hillier, Van E. Acknowledging Sources and Avoiding Plagiarism: http://uwp.duke.edu/sources.html.

History News Network: http://chnm.gmu.edu/hun.

Hunt, Lynn. "French History in the Last Twenty Years: The Rise and Fall of the *Annales* Paradigm." *Journal of Contemporary History* 21 (1986): 209–24.

Hutton, Patrick H. *History and the Art of Memory.* Hanover, NH: University Press of New England, 1993.

Iggers, George. *Historiography in the Twentieth Century: From Scientific Objectivity to the Postmodern Challenge.* Middletown, CT: Wesleyan University Press, 1997.

Institute of Historical Research, University of London, History On-Line: http://ihr.sas.ac.uk/search/welcome.html.

Jenkins, Keith. *The Postmodern History Reader.* London: Routledge, 1997.

Keegan, John. *The Battle for History: Re-fighting World War II.* New York: Vintage Books, 1995.

Kracauer, Siegfried. *History: The Last Things before the Last.* New York: Oxford University Press, 1969.

Kubler, George. *The Shape of Time.* New Haven: Yale University Press, 1962.

Library of Congress American Memory: http://memory.loc.gov/ammem/mdbquery.html.

Linenthal, Edward T., and Tom Engelhardt, eds. *History Wars: The* Enola Gay *and Other Battles for the American Past.* New York: Henry Holt, 1996.

Lipstadt, Deborah. *Denying the Holocaust: The Growing Assault on Truth and Memory.* New York: Free Press, 1993.

"The Lore of the Sharpshooter." In *Devil's Den: A History and a Guide.* Gettysburg, PA: Thomas Publications, 1997.

MacLean, Nancy. "The Leo Frank Case Reconsidered: Gender and Sexual Politics in the Making of Reactionary Populism." *Journal of American History* 78:3 (December 1991): 917–48.

Maclean, Norman. *Young Men and Fire.* Chicago: University of Chicago Press, 1992.

Making of America (Michigan): http://moa.umdl.umich.edu.

"Managing Information; Avoiding Plagiarism." In *The Bedford Handbook*, 5th ed., by Diana Hacker, pp. 554–62. Boston: Bedford Books, 1998.

Middleton, Arthur Pierce, and Douglass Adair. "The Mystery of the Horn Papers." *William and Mary Quarterly*, 3d ser., 4 (October 1947): 409–43.

Monmonier, Mark. *Mapping It Out: Expository Cartography for the Humanities and Social Sciences.* Chicago: University of Chicago Press, 1993.

National Archives and Records Administration Information Locator (NAIL): http://www.nara.gov/nara/nailhi.html.

National Union Catalogue of Manuscript Collections: http://lcweb.loc.gov/coll/nucmc.html.

Neustadt, Richard E., and Ernest R. May. *Thinking in Time: The Uses of History for Decision-Makers.* New York: Macmillan, Free Press, 1985.

Nitpickers Web site: http://www.nitpickers.com/movies/nitpicks.

Novick, Peter. *That Noble Dream: The "Objectivity Question" and the American Historical Profession.* New York: Cambridge University Press, 1988.

O'Brien, Tim. *The Things They Carried: A Work of Fiction.* New York: Penguin, 1990.

Onuf, Peter S., and Jan E. Lewis, eds. *Sally Hemings and Thomas Jefferson: History, Memory, and Civic Culture.* Charlottesville: University of Virginia Press, 1999.

Plumb, J.H. *The Death of the Past.* Boston: Houghton Mifflin, 1970.

Poster, Mark. *Cultural History and Postmodernity: Disciplinary Readings and Challenges.* New York: Columbia University Press, 1997.

Reardon, Carol. *Pickett's Charge in History and Memory.* Chapel Hill: University of North Carolina Press, 1997.

"Recognizing Plagiarism and Acknowledging Sources." In *The New St. Martin's Handbook*, by Andrea Lunsford and Robert Connors, pp. 494–97. Boston: Bedford/St. Martin's, 1999.

Rendell, Kenneth W. *Forging History: The Detection of Fake Letters and Documents.* Norman: University of Oklahoma Press, 1994.

Reviews in American History: http://muse.jhu.edu/journals/reviews_in_american_history.

Rollins, Peter C. *Hollywood as Historian.* 2d ed. Lexington: University Press of Kentucky, 1998.

Roth, Randolph. "Guns, Gun Culture, and Homicide: The Relationship between Firearms, the Uses of Firearms, and Interpersonal Violence." *William and Mary Quarterly*, 3d ser., 59:1 (January 2002): 223–40.

Schama, Simon. *Dead Certainties (Unwanted Speculations).* New York: Vintage, 1991.

Scott, Joan. *Gender and the Politics of History.* New York: Columbia University Press, 1989.

Shermer, Michael, and Alex Grobman. *Denying History: Who Says the Holocaust Never Happened and Why Do They Say It?* Berkeley: University of California Press, 2000.

Smith, Bonnie G. *The Gender of History: Men, Women, and the Practice of History.* Cambridge, MA: Harvard University Press, 1998.

Stern, Fritz J. *The Varieties of History.* New York: Meridian, 1956.

Stoianovich, Traian. *French Historical Method: The Annales Paradigm.* Ithaca, NY: Cornell University Press, 1976.

Tosh, John. *The Pursuit of History: Aims, Methods, and New Directions in the Study of Modern History.* 2d ed. London: Longman, 1991.

Toynbee, Arnold. *A Study of History.* New York: Oxford University Press, 1957.

Trinkle, Dennis A., and Scott A. Merriman, eds. *The History Highway 3.0.* Armonk, NY: M.E. Sharpe, 2002.

Weston, Anthony. *A Rulebook for Arguments.* 2d ed. Indianapolis: Hackett Publishers, 1992.

White, Hayden. *The Content of the Form: Narrative Discourse and Historical Representation.* Baltimore: Johns Hopkins University Press, 1987.

———. *Metahistory: The Historical Imagination in Nineteenth-century Europe.* Baltimore: Johns Hopkins University Press, 1973.

Whitrow, G.J. *Time in History.* Oxford: Oxford University Press, 1988.

Wilson, Norman J. *History in Crisis? Recent Directions in Historiography.* Upper Saddle River, NJ: Prentice Hall, 1999.

Windschuttle, Keith. *The Killing of History: How a Discipline Is Being Murdered by Literary Critics and Social Criticism.* Paddington, Australia: Macleay, 1996.

Winks, Robin W., ed. *The Historian as Detective.* New York: Harper and Row, 1968.

Wright, Robert. *Nonzero: The Logic of Human Destiny.* New York: Vintage, 2000.

WWW.VL History Central Catalogue: http://www.ukans.edu/history/VL/.

Zenzen, Joan. *Battling for Manassas: The Fifty-year Preservation Struggle at Manassas Battlefield Park.* State College: Pennsylvania State University Press, 1998.

Index

About the Author

Robert C. Williams is Vail Professor of History and Dean of Faculty Emeritus at Davidson College in Davidson, North Carolina. He is the author of numerous books and articles in modern Russian, American, and European history, and a founding board member of History Associates Incorporated. He previously taught at Williams College and Washington University in St. Louis.

DATE DUE

OC 15 '04			
JE 12 '05			
JY 28 '05			
SE 12 '05			
DE 18 '05			
AP 4 '06		WITHDRAWN	
MY 06 '06			
JE 18 '06			
ILL			
30380554			
6/8/07			
NO 16 '07			
JAN 0 4 2010			
JUL 3 2010			

DEMCO 38-296